To Tom
A Merry Christmas - 1972
from Mother
with Love

THE
VISCONTI
HOURS

THE
VISCONTI
HOURS

National Library, Florence

MILLARD MEISS

AND

EDITH W. KIRSCH

GEORGE BRAZILLER   NEW YORK

Alla Biblioteca Nazionale Rinata

Published in 1972. Reproduced from the Illuminated Manuscript
belonging to the National Library, Florence, Italy.
All rights reserved. No part of the contents of this book
may be reproduced without the written consent of the
publisher, George Braziller, Inc.
One Park Avenue, New York, N.Y. 10016
Library of Congress Catalog Card Number: 72–75371
Standard Book Number: 0–8076–0651–0
Printed in France by Draeger Frères, Paris.
Bound in Switzerland by Mayer and Soutter

CONTENTS

Acknowledgments

The authors thank Dottoressa A. M. Giorgetti Vichi, Director of the National Library, Florence; Dottoressa Eugenia Levi, formerly Keeper of Manuscripts; and Dottore Filippo di Benedetto, Keeper of Manuscripts, for their constant helpfulness during the preparation of this book.

INTRODUCTION

I

I first saw part of the Visconti Hours early in 1947. Arriving at the Uffizi after a walk past the shattered buildings and the rubble of war, I entered the office of the Superintendent of Galleries, who put the manuscript, recently acquired by the city of Florence, in my hands. He wanted to still for a moment our talk of destruction, and he certainly succeeded. Turning the pages of this little-known book, I was surprised and enchanted by the uniqueness of its art. Not only was it unlike anything I had ever seen; it could not possibly have been predicted from the paintings that preceded it. Its marvelous extravagance seemed all the more impressive amidst the sobriety of Florentine art—but perhaps the giants of Michelangelo are really an extravagance of another kind.

The manuscript, which Baron Horace Finaly had just given to Florence, is the second part of an exceptionally rich Book of Hours. It was illuminated by two quite different artists. Giovannino dei Grassi and his workshop painted the first folios for Giangaleazzo Visconti, despot of Milan. Giangaleazzo's death in 1402 interrupted the lagging work, and it was resumed by Belbello da Pavia for Giangaleazzo's son Filippo Maria, after he became Duke in 1412. Many people prefer Belbello's illumination to Giovannino's, but I have always inclined to the reverse, so that I later welcomed an opportunity to see the little-known first part of the prayer book, still in the possession of the Visconti family, because I knew that all of it was illuminated by Giovannino and his assistants. My admiration of the imaginative forms and scintillating color, which I attempted to communicate in print in 1967, did not diminish during subsequent visits. When, therefore, in 1969 the eminent paleographer and director of the Biblioteca Nazionale, Emanuele Casamassima, told me that this first part, separated from the second for centuries, had been acquired by the State and would be reunited with it in his library, I felt deeply pleased, all the more because the acquisition at this time, in the aftermath of the devastating flood, was one more sign that the great Florentine library would not only recover but grow. I accepted immediately his invitation to undertake a facsimile that would bring to a large audience this extraordinary work.*

LF 57v Giangaleazzo Visconti, who commissioned the Book of Hours, was the most ambitious and probably the cleverest member of a powerful family. The Visconti, who liked to trace their descent from Venus and Anchises, ruled Milan for more than a century. Giangaleazzo, born in 1351, married no less a person than Isabelle, daughter of King John of France. Their daughter Valentina became the wife of Louis d'Orléans, younger brother of King Charles VI of France, so that Giangaleazzo was doubly linked with the French royal family. French literature and French art were highly esteemed at his court.

Giangaleazzo became the sole ruler of the County of Milan in 1385. He launched a campaign of territorial expansion that brought all Lombardy and Emilia under his rule and carried his power to the gates of Florence. He cultivated the favor of the German Emperor, and in 1395 Wenceslaus granted him an honor and privilege denied to all his predecessors: his deputy crowned him Duke and hereditary ruler of Milan. Since the text of the Book of Hours refers to Giangaleazzo as Count it was definitely written before the coronation of 1395. Furthermore, the imperial eagle that he henceforth proudly displayed does not appear among his emblems, so most if not all the illumination accomplished for him must antedate 1395 also.

Giangaleazzo became the sole ruler of Milan in 1385 only by disposing of his uncle, Bernabò, who was also his second wife's father. His concern for the acceptance of his authority led him quite naturally to display his heraldic devices and mottoes on all occasions. They abound even in his prayer book made primarily for private use. These armorials often radiate light as dazzling as the symbols of God and the saints. The arms and devices of a prince do not of course provide a deep or intriguing subject for a painter, not to mention his later audience. No one has maintained, however, that the public life of Marie de Medici is enormously edifying, yet Rubens made of these unpromising episodes a glorious pictorial cycle.

BR 105, 115, 128 In addition to the armorials Giangaleazzo himself is represented three times. Unlike another contemporary prince, the Duke of Berry, who also enjoyed seeing himself portrayed in his Books of Hours, Giangaleazzo does not appear in prayer before the Madonna or a saint. His head alone is depicted in a medallion unrelated to the religious scenes, though on BR 105 he does seem to be looking across to the *Annunciation* on the facing page. When adopting a portrait of this kind Giovannino had as models similar portraits in the frescoes of

---

*The manuscript is in two volumes bearing the signatures (B)anco (R)ari 397 and (L)andau (F)inaly 22.

Altichiero and in Veronese manuscripts. He was probably familiar also with ancient coins and medals. Indeed, on one folio of the Visconti Hours he introduced two profile heads of Roman emperors. LF 51

Though during his rather brief period of rule from 1385 to his death in 1402 Giangaleazzo devoted himself primarily to the expansion of his political power, he found time for other occupations. When not directing the capture of neighboring states or populations he hunted wild animals, some of which are depicted on the pages of his prayer book. Not inappropriately his profile head on folio 115 is framed by a hunting dog and a stag. Trained birds of prey populate the borders. The illuminator, catching the spirit, envisaged even the psalmist David as a hunter.

BR 48, 105; LF 41 BR 120v

In addition to hunting and war Giangaleazzo undertook enterprises with more durable results. He built, or rebuilt, several castles, and he supported the construction of the enormous Cathedral of Milan. Some North Europeans were engaged in the work and in 1399 a major French painter, Jacques Coene (perhaps the Boucicaut Master), came down to join the builders. In 1396 the Duke laid the cornerstone for the famous Certosa of Pavia.

Like other tyrants in Ferrara, Mantua, and Urbino, Giangaleazzo patronized learning and the arts. He took an interest in the University of Pavia, which his father had founded. The Roman humanist Poggio praised the scholars at his court. Giangaleazzo continued to build the great library at Pavia that his predecessors had begun. Indeed, in the late fourteenth century he made this city and Milan major European centers for the production of illuminated manuscripts. By giving special attention to this art he followed in the footsteps of his relatives, the Valois princes in France, the greatest of all patrons and collectors of illuminated books. From the Lombard workshops, however, came a distinctive and indeed unique series of splendid illustrated books devoted to plants, animals, medicine, and climate. Small wonder that a remarkable copy of the great ancient treatise, Pliny's *Natural History*, a major source of this interest, was illuminated at Pavia in 1389.

Giovannino dei Grassi fully shared this delight in nature. He filled his borders and occasionally his initials with animals and birds, all of them attentively studied and affectionately rendered. Many of them, such as deer, rabbits, dogs, cranes, hoopoe, are native. Giangaleazzo's zoo no doubt sheltered others—cheetahs, lions, peacocks, and parakeets. The illuminator very skillfully portrayed also butterflies, flies and beetles, and occasionally flowers, such as the white daisies on BR 128.

BR 2v, 22v, 35v, 48, 108v, 115, 124v, 147v; LF 19, 30

In all this Giovannino dei Grassi was influenced by the Lombard intellectual milieu, but before him the depiction of fauna and flora had progressed in secular rather than in religious books. He himself did not of course achieve such extraordinary results for the first time and all at once on the pages of the Visconti Hours. He had been studying animals for years, and he carefully recorded the sum of his observations on parchment in a little book of models that by good luck still survives in Bergamo. Some of the creatures drawn by him in this book (lesser artists added a number) appear likewise in the Visconti Hours.

BR 2v   Giovannino lost no opportunity to introduce animals into religious scenes where they might be appropriate. Thus in the representation of the childless Joachim after his rejection from the Temple the farm includes not only the usual sheep but a herd of cattle. Two of these animals drink from a gushing spring, another turns its head to nip one of the flies that torments it. An old shepherd, scantily clothed, is comfortably lodged in a crevice, and another, with torn and patched tunic, looks up at the deeply disconsolate Joachim. The watchdog, sensing no trouble, lies asleep. The animals and shepherds are described to a much greater extent from life—from actual models—than the saint and the angel, whose drapery ripples and flows in accordance with the conventions of the time. Indeed this hillside scene, which gives us a glimpse even of the thatched shelter of the shepherds perched on a peak, evokes pastoral life so vividly that Joachim's long blue mantle, though splendid, seems inappropriate and highly impractical.

LF 19   The worldly ramifications of spiritual history, more or less prominent in the miniatures, often become the main subjects of the rest of the folio. A fascinating example is LF 19, where within the initial D (*Deus*) the Lord creates heaven and earth. Hovering over "the face of the deep," a layer of undifferentiated blue substance from which emerge a few angels' heads, God raises His hands in a gesture of command. An angel kneeling on top of a tower in the right margin bears a large book inscribed with the verses from Genesis: "In the beginning God created the heaven and the earth." In the ellipse of green earth encircling the Lord monks, seated near churches, hold open books and contemplate the words that presumably refer to creation. Specimens of God's handiwork are scattered over the folio: flies, an ape, falcons, a beetle, a butterfly, a hoopoe, and four deer.

    The beautiful capital letters in the manuscript, alive with creatures of all kinds, may, as we have just seen, extend the religious meaning of the miniatures they enclose, but more often they constitute zones of worldly life. On BR 147v, around the scene of the Virgin Mary with the infant Baptist and Elizabeth, the letter M—the initial of *Magnificat*—is filled with four maidens who play catch amidst the swirling leaves. The white rabbits below, common symbols of fertility,

10

might refer to the pregnancy of the Virgin and the recent birth of the Baptist. The border that surrounds the beginning of this important canticle is especially rich and glows with an abundance of simplified flowers. In the initials that surround the biblical scenes the patron himself comes close to the divine. In the illustration on BR 23 of the Psalm, "The Lord is my Light," David appears within an initial D formed in part by the terrifying Visconti emblem of the *biscia*—the twisting serpent that devours an infant. The coils of the monster, winding around the first letter of the Lord's name, surround Him and the psalmist. The same emblem on a much smaller scale ornaments the banners flown in the margin by angels, God's emissaries. Giangaleazzo's right to rule, we are thus assured, is divine, although in actuality he secured sole power only by a violent act. Angels again bear the *biscia*, flying down from heaven, on LF 4v. On Br 122v they hold his motto; on 36 and 76v it serves as a border.

Some of Giangaleazzo's emblems are identical with those that have the highest religious connotations. Their meaning, therefore, is determined entirely by the context. Thus the sun, which envelops the Madonna and Child in the vision of Aracoeli, is more often an emblem of the Count. A white dove may be either the Holy Ghost or another device of the patron. Since his first wife, a daughter of the French king, brought as part of her dowry the Comté de Vertus in the Champagne, Giangaleazzo—profiting from the power of words in the Middle Ages—became the Count of Virtues, *Comes virtutum*, and he adopted as emblems the Cardinal Virtues.

BR 150v

BR 104v, 105, 128

BR 108v, 120v; LF 17

Although the scribe who wrote the text of the prayer book signed his name, Frater Amadeus, the illuminators are, as usual at this time, silent about their identity, and only other evidence tells us that it was the imagination of Giovannino dei Grassi to which we owe the designs of the first part of this manuscript. This master was first mentioned in 1389, as a painter in the workshops of the Cathedral. In 1391 the records show he exercised a general authority as "capomaestro," and he is also qualified as a sculptor.[1] A large relief in the Cathedral representing the *Noli me tangere*, made at this time, has often been attributed to at least his design.[2] It seems, however, so stiff and dry that I question whether the artist responsible for the other objects more firmly connected with Giovannino can have provided anything but a preliminary drawing. In 1395 Giovannino was designing capitals for the Cathedral, and he employed as assistant his brother Porrone. One of the few excellent pages in the pattern-book in Bergamo, to which we have referred, bears a very old inscription attesting the authorship of Giovannino dei Grassi, and historians agree that this draftsman must be the author of the best folios in the Visconti Hours.

11

Such a conclusion is confirmed by the one other fact we possess. In 1396 the Works of the Cathedral commissioned a Breviary, and in August 1398 payments for the illumination were made to the survivor of the illuminators, Salomone dei Grassi, Giovannino's son. Giovannino himself, the record states, had died July 6.[3]

This Breviary still exists, in the Biblioteca Trivulziana in Milan. It is closer in style than any other manuscript to the Visconti Hours. No less telling is the fact that the borders resemble especially what we may describe as the second phase of the dei Grassi style in the Visconti Hours. This phase begins on folio 9 of LF, and it is distinguished by the prevalence of gold vines and leaves, no doubt reflecting renewed French influence, and by pastel colors, especially pale rose and blue. The margins of subsequent folios frequently contain large structural LF 54, 17, forms, powerful vines, a pair of trees, or more often towers. The latter 19 appear frequently also in the Breviary, and they seem to reflect Giovannino's activity during the nineties as supervisor of construction and designer of architectural details. Very little in the Breviary equals the best drawings in the pattern-book or the strongest illumination in the first part of the Visconti Hours, and the same must be said of much—but certainly not all—of the painting in the dei Grassi style in LF. We shall refer to these brilliant exceptions shortly.

Our inference about chronology, with which not all specialists would agree,[4] is that the latest work of Giovannino and his associates in the Visconti Hours should be dated in the nineties, probably but not certainly before 1395, when Giangaleazzo was crowned duke. At that time the huge enterprise was proceeding slowly if at all because of Giovannino's commitments to the Cathedral. It was then abandoned because he died in 1398 and Giangaleazzo followed him to the grave in 1402. The manuscript, its illumination only about half-complete, lay about until Duke Filippo Maria later asked Belbello da Pavia to finish it.

If the dei Grassi were still working on the Visconti Hours in the nineties, when did they begin? Here we strike a highly controversial BR 2 issue, because the base of the temple from which Joachim is expelled bears a date, probably 1370, written in the same red pigment that was used on the surrounding surface. It could therefore signify, as some scholars maintain, the date of the execution of this miniature and others like it, though the reason for the choice of this building for the inscription is not clear. The miniatures on these folios, however, and still more the spectacular borders, would not only be unique in 1370 but they have no reflections in Lombard illumination until the end of the century. Only then, in manuscripts such as a Missal in the Biblioteca Ambrosiana, the *Historia Plantarum* in the Casanatense, and the

12

Hours of Isabel of Castille in The Hague, did the illuminators of Milan and Pavia reveal an awareness of the stupendous innovations of Giovannino. Presumably, then, Giovannino began work on the Visconti Hours in the later eighties. This inference from the course of Milanese illumination coincides with the fascinating iconographic and historical evidence for this date offered by Edith Kirsch in her part of this introduction.

Earlier relationships between Giovannino and other Lombard masters there of course were. They concern, however, the less original aspects of his art, and they therefore may just as well indicate what he learned as what he gave. The segmented gold frames of his miniatures, consisting of lozenges and squares interspersed among longer pointed bands, were employed by the illuminator of a Book of Hours in the Biblioteca Estense in Modena datable about 1390. Giovannino's figures resemble those of the well-known illuminator of the Book of Hours and Missal in the Bibliothèque nationale, lat. 757, and of Smith–Lesouëf 22 in the same library, both datable ca. 1380. These manuscripts belong to the central trend of Lombard illumination, as we see it first in the seventies in the manuscripts of Giovanni di Benedetto da Como and as late as 1395 in the Missal illuminated by Anovelo da Imbonate as part of the celebration of Giangaleazzo's coronation.

The miniatures of these masters all transfer the pictorial conventions of Lombard fresco painting to the pages of a book with far less change than they undergo in the Visconti Hours. Even the outstanding contemporary of Giovannino, the illuminator of the superb *Giron le courtois* in Paris, who did experiment with the relationship of picture and page by diminishing contrasts of color and introducing new kinds of frames, nevertheless retained to a greater degree the figures and the compositions of monumental painting. Indeed, painting on panel and on the wall attracted the major artists throughout central and northern Italy in the fourteenth century so that, with the exception of Giovannino, illumination remained a secondary art. It tended to adopt norms established for painting on a different ground, in a different context, and on a far greater scale.

Giovannino dei Grassi was the first Italian painter of the fourteenth century who created an entirely distinctive style of illumination. His extraordinary achievement, due primarily to a special kind of genius, was at the same time facilitated by circumstances peculiar to Milan. Indeed, with the full use of hindsight, one might say that Giangaleazzo's court among all Italian centers was destined to witness a unique efflorescence of the art of the book. He provided special patronage, first of all, for the library founded by his immediate predecessors, developing it into one of the greatest collections in Europe, equal in size and splendor to those of his Valois relatives in France. For him, furthermore, as for the Valois princes (except the Burgundian dukes), illumination was more attractive than panel painting. We know, in fact, practically no Milanese panels of the last quarter of the fourteenth century or the first quarter of the fifteenth.

Painting in manuscripts therefore provided special opportunities and offered special rewards in Milan. Giovannino, feeling more independent of the canons established elsewhere in panel painting, was freer to evolve an art peculiarly for the book. In making this attempt he learned much from the two most distinctive and beautiful manuscript styles in contemporary Europe, the French and the Bohemian. Books produced in those centers were not lacking in Milan, and they enjoyed a special prestige as productions of the regions with which Giangaleazzo was most closely allied. Surely Giovannino learned from the "Boqueteaux" illuminators in Paris how to evoke vibrant figures and landscapes with an open brushwork of small spots and widely spaced strokes. Not only this aspect of his art, as we see it for instance on LF 30, but also the linear vitality and the clustering of trees and flowers recall the great Master of the Bible of Jean de Sy. Furthermore, as the late Professor Arslan demonstrated a decade ago, other aspects of Giovannino's style, such as his initials in which figures are embedded in leaves, stems, or tubes of the same color, were inspired by Bohemian models.

see Paris, Bibl. nat., lat. 6540–6541 Beginning with a border of vine and ivy in gold, blue, and red, characteristically French but outmoded there in the late fourteenth century, Lombard illuminators often achieved highly distinctive and impressive designs. Only Giovannino, however, transformed all his models to the degree that he initiated a true mutation in the book. On each folio he employed, to begin with, relatively few colors—primarily blue and red—which he modulated with an exceptional taste and sensitiveness. He set pale blue near deep ultramarine, and pink, mauve, russet, and violet near a sonorous red, occasionally intermingled with touches of green and an exquisite yellow. He enriched these pigments with three kinds of gold. Many forms, such as the stars strewn over the folios, were painted with gold emulsion, and they have a relatively matte surface. Giovannino employed much gold leaf also, burnishing it to provide a bright sheen. Most exceptional of all, he glazed the gold in a transparent oil red. No other illuminator anywhere exploited equally these different metallic effects. Their endlessly varied combination with the usual pigments constitutes perhaps the chief glory of the manuscript.

This view of Giovannino's accomplishments would not have

been shared a generation later by the author of the earliest known treatise on painting, Leone Battista Alberti. Wishing to promote a new estimate of the artist and his work, Alberti insisted that it was artistry that counted, not precious materials. He opposed the use of gold in painting. Since this metal had been employed extensively in medieval art it symbolized, too, many values that he wished to supplant. Despite his injunction and the apparent concurrence of some artists in Florence, other painters did not hesitate to employ gold—there was even a revival of it in the later fifteenth century—until lowered tones and deepened shadows made it entirely incongruous. Though it was later applied outside the pictorial field, to frames, sculptures, and other surfaces, there developed a sort of inverted snobbery, as though gold were necessarily associated with meretriciousness, a clear sign of artistic inferiority.

Obviously, however, the mere presence of a precious and inherently beautiful metal does not necessarily diminish the quality of a painting, any more than the use of polished marble assures a poorer building than rough concrete. Gold, furthermore, is not the only precious material employed by artists; like countless other paintings the Visconti Hours contains silver and lapis lazuli, a beautiful, rare, and always a very expensive kind of blue. Gold (or silver), to be sure, differs from other colors by being more reflective, particularly when laid as leaf and burnished. Giovannino, however, employs shining surfaces of this kind for certain limited effects, and he tames gold, so to speak, by glazing it or dulling it in an emulsion. Surely it is not so much gold itself as these metallic modulations and their interplay with other colors that give his pages their unique character and beauty.

Giovannino reserved the greatest brilliance for his borders. No two of them are alike. Each is a surprise, and the illuminator's inexhaustible imagination here shows its greatest originality. He wanted literally to light up the text, the religious episodes, and the emblems of his patron, setting them in a sea of precious, scintillating objects. His blazing folios resemble jewelry and enamels more than the painted pages of contemporary masters. They are as iridescent and tangible BR 2, 112v as necklaces or earrings. His accomplishment soon impressed illuminators in France, especially the Boucicaut Master, but Giovannino alone commonly employed oil glaze in the borders as well as in the miniatures and only he combined it with so many other luminary devices. His ever-changing, refulgent red-gold remained unique in the history of the book.

In other respects, too, the folios of the Visconti Hours resemble the products of contemporary goldsmiths, especially those French *joyaux* composed of glistening enamels and precious stones. On folio

15

48v the miniature, with its gold background and sparkling golden ornaments, is enclosed by the clear Delft blue of the tubular initial. This in turn is animated by numerous small huts, projecting roofs, white rabbits and the dark holes from which they emerge. Then the gold rectangle outside is filled with rows of tiny shields, creating an effect like that of the nearby letters against the white parchment. Giovannino delights in the vibration produced here and throughout the manuscript by the multiplication of small forms. He followed in this respect the conventional Gothic diaper, but instead of employing simply squares, rectangles, or lozenges he sets in serried array tiny Visconti shields, suns, flowers, and small crowns. Occasionally, as on folio 136, the same unit—the lozenge—that is multiplied outside the miniature is strewn over a religious figure within it, though in a different color. This repetition discloses both the degree of the painter's abstraction and his ability to harmonize two divergent modes of representation, the more purely formal and the naturalistic.

BR 48v, 145, 122v, 36

Similar small shapes sparkle beyond the initials, in the borders; and then they escape, so to speak, into the empty fields outside. Here they shine like golden stars, transforming the surface of the folio into a diaphanous plane. Their rays which light the area around conform in general to one pattern, but they are irregularly and very freely drawn. Each star is thus slightly different from its neighbors, adding to the excitement of the page. They are diminutive variants of the large suns, bright gold or translucent red, which are more regular in design but extremely active in the bold waviness of their rays.

The little stars embody a principle that is basic to Giovannino's art. Somewhat as in Gothic architecture, forms progress from the solid to the tenuous, from the defined to the unbounded, from the static to the active. Often, as on LF 26, the only still, self-contained form is God, painted in sober gray-blue and pink. From Him emanate, however, red seraphs, golden flames and rays. The progression is repeated in the tubular initial. It swells and shrinks, vibrates with small pointed forms, and sends forth through leaflike rays a force that seems to electrify the entire page. The charge, originating in God, brings forth sparks from the leaves throughout the border. On BR 108v it is David who is at the center of a ring of rays, which end in sparkling droplets of gold scattered over the page. On BR 3 David's spectacular red glazed aureole emits long painted gold rays. In response there are lesser bursts in the border.

These dazzling luminary displays recall the sculptural compositions, on a far larger scale, of Bernini, though he is able to utilize light itself as a source. Giovannino's bursting and transitory forms are closer still to fireworks. Here too substance is transformed into light,

16

and only the sound is missing.

Sometimes solid golden arabesques run off into rivulets. Leaves BR 48v
of gold foil seem to dissolve into sparks. On several folios Giovannino BR 22v
devised the ancestor in art of the pinwheel, an exciting pyrotechnical BR 36
device that shoots out colored light as it spins. The painter ascribes
this energy to profane as well as to religious sources, although the religious content still holds the central position on the page. The portrait
of Giangaleazzo or his motto and emblems often create a secondary
display in the borders, surrounded as they are by the device of the
sun, which is identical with the aureole of God or of David.

The principle of progression from the solid to the tenuous governs
also the treatment of the text. The lines of script opposite the initial
often alternate with bands of golden filigree. The entire column of BR 115
text, lightly bounded by three pale gray lines, is then dissolved, so to
speak, into lively golden tracery. The script hovers with perfect con-
sistency in the luminous field of the page. On many folios, furthermore, which have denser borders, red ink is employed to harmonize
them with the text. The web of lines around the borders has the same BR 120v, 136
effect as the gold tracery around the text.

Giovannino's marvelous improvisation with color and light is
accompanied by an unflagging inventiveness with patterns. He delights in creating novel ornaments. His arabesques, as on BR 146v,
never fail to show a buoyant vitality. The posture and the scroll of
Zachariah on this page also give abundant proof of his rhythmical
power.

This force diminishes, however, in the second section of the manuscript, which we judge to have been begun after an interval. To be
sure, Giovannino employed assistants already in the first part: entire
folios, even one with a portrait of the Count, are obviously inferior. BR 76, 128
He himself participated less in the second part, but his ideas are present, and sometimes his hand. His colors, as on LF 17, tend to be paler, LF 17
he uses more white, and he strives for a quieter, less scintillating, more
lyrical effect. The folio has a firmer general structure. Golden acorns
fall from the two oak trees, one pale pink, one blue; they are scattered
across the white parchment like the stars, though not quite equal in
radiance. Compared to earlier representations of the sun the one on
this folio is frail and spidery. The two pasty doves at the sides of it
were surely inserted by an assistant. The general blandness of the folio
makes all the more effective the burst of glorious color in the oak
leaves. The buff, pale green, blue, pink, red, and black compose a soft,
luminous autumn bouquet of a very rare beauty.

The initial takes up the theme of the folio, but with a modified
design and in much higher color. Two slender trees, entwined by a

vine bearing large white flowers, frame the bishop saints. The central tree, which forms the vertical bar of the letter T (*Te Deum*), is a great oak which, like those in the margins, sends forth leaves or suckers along its trunk. It is more naturalistically rendered, however, with a crinkly brown trunk and pale green leaves. Above, three branches spread to each side, their leaves whitened by the light as they move across the highly burnished gold ground. They compose the horizontal bar of the T and at the same time a bower for each of the saints. They might almost be the ribs of vaults or the tracery of glass windows, reminding us of the later association of Gothic architecture and trees.

LF 30   On folio 30 little Gothic towers and chapels actually nestle in the branches of the trees. They emerge from clusters of flowers, as a kind of special fruit. Close to the main trunk, alongside primitive shelters, two hermits sit holding their books. The weight and volume of the buildings are transmuted in Giovannino's inimitable way. The flowers around them are highly animated, and they put forth innumerable golden "stamens" that radiate life and light into the open space around. Though the trees on this folio have strong roots and stout trunks, they are made of gold, and thus they maintain both the real and the fantastic aspects of the design. Irrational as these structures may be, they are realized with so wonderful a taste and tact that we delight in their imaginativeness without doubting their probability.

We can retrace on this folio the paths of Giovannino's fantasy. The initial D (*Deus*) again repeats the themes of the borders, but in a more concentrated and dynamic way. The golden branches grow out of a small gray-blue mountain that reposes on the solid but flowery capital letters of the Psalm. The miniature shows the Lord separating the land from the water, and streams indeed seem to run out over the land before our very eyes. The ornamental band between the lines of text echoes this movement by rippling in waves across the page. Giovannino plays with the theme of creation and of water by inserting into the initial two primitive, therefore naked people (male and female? Adam and Eve?) who carry a canteen and a barrel.

The newly formed land supports two simple sheds. They are apparently shelters for men who live a primitive life, and indeed three hermits gather for discussion in the landscape below. A lean-to like those above rises on the rock at the left. It shelters, however, an ox! What the holy hermits discuss is not clear, but they are already menaced by the appearance of evil in the world. Toward them moves a devilish dragon with a charming head: the head of the original temptress in the Garden. Behind her rises a chapel similar to one in the trees, and it seems probable that the idea of newly integrated land suggested hermits to Giovannino, as the water had inspired the canteens, and then hermits as well as hermitages rose into the trees.

In the empty space above the tree at the left, at the inner side of the folio, a curious structure appears, bearing anomalously a small, gabled shed. The structure itself is round and woven, looking like a beehive, but out of it emerges a golden grapevine that bears green leaves and a bunch of golden grapes. Its presence here is mysterious. Is it another form of primitive shelter? Could the painter have associated the "stamens," the countless tiny gold squares that cluster around the flowers, with bees?

The imaginative art of Giovannino dei Grassi survives in this book alone. In it he combines an entirely personal vision of light radiating from saints and prophets—and from the Duke of Milan also—with an equally original exploration of the natural world. He impresses us more perhaps when depicting the creatures of God than God Himself. The Duke shared Giovannino's enthusiasm for animals, but the hunter's interest culminated in aggression and death, the painter's in affectionate re-creation. Those who contemplate the pages of this book will find in them one of the gayest, most spontaneous, and most fanciful talents of Western illumination.

II

STRUCTURE

The Visconti Hours is the preeminent Italian example of the numerous surviving Books of Hours produced during the late Middle Ages, mainly in countries north of Italy, for the private devotional use of wealthy lay persons. Books of Hours derive their name from their essential component, the Hours of the Virgin, also called the Little Office of the Blessed Virgin Mary. The supplementary components of these books vary. Many include additional offices (devotional texts) dedicated to the Deity, to saints, to holy events or objects, and to the dead; like the Hours of the Virgin, these offices are divided for recitation at fixed times of the day known as canonical hours. Most Books of Hours contain also a liturgical calendar, the seven Penitential Psalms, a Litany (ritual invocations for the mercy of the Trinity and the intercession of the saints), and Suffrages (prayers to saints especially venerated by the owner of the manuscript). Although the Visconti Hours has no Calendar and Suffrages, it is augmented by a full Psalter, including canticles, hymns, and other prayers which normally follow the Psalms, and therefore belongs to a category of books which are designated Psalter-Hours.[5]

The text of the Visconti Hours is arranged as follows:

Banco Rari 397:

Psalms I–CL (except CXLII, which may have been omitted inadvertently by the scribe)	Folios 1–144v (fols. 1–2v contain full-page miniatures)
Canticle of the Three Hebrews	145–146
Canticle of Zacharias	146v–147
Magnificat	147v–148
Te Deum	148v–149v
Conclusion of *Gloria in Excelsis* (the original preceding leaf, whose recto probably contained the Canticle of Simeon, has been cut out of the manuscript—see the commentary for BR 148v)	150
Lord's Prayer	150v
Apostles' Creed	151–151v

*

21

Landau–Finaly 22 (folio 57 is blank; folios not listed below contain full-page miniatures):

Evidence of various kinds indicates that the two volumes of the book were originally intended as one. The leaves, though all have been trimmed, are approximately the same size; each full text page in both volumes contains twenty-one lines which occupy the same amount of space on all pages, and the script of both parts appears to have been written by the same scribe at the same time.[6] The first three textual components of LF 22 (Athanasian Creed, Penitential Psalms, and Litany) would be appropriate at the conclusion of a Psalter (BR 397), whereas the duplicate set of Penitential Psalms and Litany belongs properly to the Hours. The presence on conjugate leaves (LF 9 and 15, 10 and 14) of parts of the first Litany and the Hours of the Virgin (see the list of gatherings on p. 258), proves that they also were intended to be in the same volume. Continuity of the pictorial cycle of the Virgin further demonstrates the unity of the two volumes: because the *Annunciation* appears in the Psalter (BR 104v), it does not occur in its customary position at the beginning of the Hours of the Virgin; the latter text is introduced instead by the *Visitation* and the *Nativity* (LF 10v, 11).

Examination of the sewing holes of the two volumes suggests, however, that they were in fact never bound together.[7] Early separation of the two parts of the book probably resulted from the failure of Giovannino's workshop to complete the decoration of the manuscript. Their work, which ends on LF 54, is sporadic even in the early gatherings of this volume, and Belbello's intervention appears probable in the punched gold background behind the initial on the first folio (see

22

the commentary for LF 1). Because of the potential usefulness of the completed portion of the Psalter as an independent text, it may have been bound before the illumination of the rest of the manuscript was finished.

ICONOGRAPHY

The subjects of the historiated initials which introduce the various sections of the Visconti Psalter are conventional. Apparently unprecedented, however, is the presence in the Psalter cycle for Matins of a second series of full-page paintings depicting the history of the Virgin.[8] This pictorial sequence begins with ten episodes from the life of Mary's parents before her birth and concludes with the annunciation to the Virgin that she will bear the Son of God. The Mariological narrative is completed in the Hours of the Virgin in LF 22 where her role in the infancy of Christ and the closing events of her life are portrayed. Here, the infancy scenes, the Virgin's death, and her coronation are iconographically traditional, but additional miniatures illustrating the annunciation of Mary's death and her funeral are unusually expansive and further emphasize her prominence in the book.

The inclusion in the Visconti manuscript of an exceptionally full cycle of the life of the Virgin, emphasizing especially the role of her parents, suggests an extraordinary devotion of Giangaleazzo to her. In fact such a relationship did exist. By 1387 the Count was concerned with construction of the Cathedral of Milan. Intended to rival and surpass the greatest Gothic cathedrals in Europe, this church was to be dedicated to the Virgin Mary. According to Bernardino Corio, whose history of Milan was first published in 1503, Giangaleazzo vowed to dedicate also to the Virgin any sons born to him.[9] For dynastic purposes the Milanese ruler needed a male heir. A widower, he had married his cousin Caterina Visconti in 1380. The first eight years of their marriage were childless. On April 8, 1387, Giangaleazzo had ratified the marriage contract between Valentina, his only surviving child by his first marriage, and Louis of Valois, brother of King Charles VI of France.[10] The agreement stipulated that Valentina was to inherit all her father's dominions if he left no sons to succeed him. More than a century later these terms were used to justify the invasion of Milan by the French army of Louis XII.

Nevertheless, Visconti succession to Milan seemed assured on September 7, 1388, by the birth of a son to Giangaleazzo and Caterina named, in fulfillment of the vow, Giovanni Maria. All the cities of the realm celebrated the event with the firing of cannons, ringing of bells, and lighting of torches. The General Council of Pavia made a gift to Caterina of a gilt bowl and one thousand florins. Milan decreed an annual holiday to commemorate the advent of an heir.[11] It seems probable that Giangaleazzo's Book of Hours was also begun to celebrate the birth of his son as well as to honor the child's patroness.

Such a purpose would explain not only the uncommon presence of a cycle of the Virgin in the Psalter, but also its unique emphasis upon episodes in the life of her parents. Giangaleazzo might have seen numerous similarities between Joachim and himself: both were wealthy, pious, and charitable; both for many years were disappointed in their wish for children; and both vowed divine dedication of the offspring for whom they prayed. The miniatures themselves seem to confirm an association between the Count of Virtues and the father of the Virgin, and a date of about 1388 for the commencement of the manuscript coincides with evidence of style presented by Professor Meiss in the first part of this introduction.

BR 1–3

Although the unconventional iconography of the Visconti Psalter is probably explicable in terms of patronage, the presence of an extensive pictorial narrative of the Old Testament in the Hours remains baffling as well as unique. A decision must have been made even before the manuscript was written to continue in the Hours of the Virgin the pattern begun in the Psalter of introducing each major subdivision of the text by a full-page miniature as well as an historiated initial. Whereas the initials in the Psalter, however, are directly appropriate to the Psalms and the other prayers which they introduce, most of those in the Hours are unrelated to the text they illustrate. Pictorial allusions to original sin as the occurrence which resulted in the need for redemption are not uncommon in Hours of the Virgin, and this association is made explicit in the Visconti Hours by the facing miniatures which portray on one side the Coronation of the Virgin and on the other the Fall of Adam and Eve (LF 50v, 51). Unusual, however, is the detailed representation of events preceding original sin, including not only the episodes of Creation, but even the Fall of the Rebel Angels (LF 12), which brought about God's decision to create man.

LF 19, 26, 30, 51, 54

That the cycles of the Creation and Fall of Man were planned during the campaign of illumination by the dei Grassi may be inferred from their authorship of several miniatures in the series. Because all evidence of dei Grassi participation in the manuscript ends on LF 54, it is more difficult to judge when the decision was made to continue the pictorial narrative of the Old Testament, not only with additional Genesis scenes illustrating the Propers for Advent in the Office of the

24

Virgin, but also with a consecutive sequence, in the following texts, of paintings drawn from subsequent books of the Bible. Thus the Office of the Dead, normally illustrated by scenes of death, interment, funeral services, and afterlife, is adorned instead in the Visconti Hours by a picture story of Exodus (only the Baptism of Christ which introduces this Office on LF 80 is conventional to the text). Scenes from the Book of Numbers decorate the Penitential Psalms and the Litany, and episodes from Deuteronomy, Joshua, Judges, and the First Book of Kings supplant the manifestations of the Holy Spirit (such as Pentecost) and the events of Christ's Passion which traditionally illustrate the Hours of the Holy Ghost, the Passion, and the Cross. Although occasionally a biblical scene in the Visconti Hours is related to the passage it illustrates, there appears to be no systematic typological relationship between the texts in the manuscript and the series of Old Testament miniatures which accompanies them.

LF 110, 156v

The Visconti biblical cycle is remarkable for its fullness. Numerous chapters are illustrated in sequence from the Books of Genesis, Exodus, Numbers, Joshua, and Judges, and sometimes (for example, LF 118 and 123v) even sequential verses within the same chapter are depicted. The absence of illustration from Leviticus and the presence of only two miniatures from Deuteronomy (LF 128, 128v) is not surprising in the context of biblical illustration as a whole: books whose contents are primarily dogmatic are normally less fully illustrated than those rich in narrative content. Because of its brevity, the Book of Ruth, which is omitted from the Visconti Hours, is sparingly illustrated even in complete Bibles.

Although in some instances Belbello and his assistants seem to have transferred motifs from one scene to another (see, for example, the commentaries for LF 127v and 128v), it is highly improbable that they invented the numerous Old Testament scenes in the Hours, using as their only pictorial model a pattern book of figure and architectural types. On the contrary, the density with which Belbello's miniatures tell their story indicates that a fully illustrated biblical narrative must have been available to him. Numerous abundantly illustrated *Bibles historiales* (Bibles based on a late thirteenth-century biblical history in French by Guyart Desmoulins) were illuminated in France during the fourteenth and fifteenth centuries. That these manuscripts were known in Italy is demonstrated by the survival of a *Bible historiale* illuminated by Belbello for Niccolò III d'Este, Marquis of Ferrara (Vatican, Barb. Lat. 613). The Visconti miniatures do not, however, coincide iconographically with their counterparts in the Bible; nor is the pictorial narrative in the Bible as full as the sequence in the Hours. On the other hand, the Visconti miniatures depict only a fraction of the episodes represented in two Bibles produced in Bohemia in the late fourteenth and early fifteenth centuries for King Wenceslaus and the master of his mint, Konrad von Vechta.[12] Still more extensively illustrated than the Bohemian manuscripts are the surviving parts of a picture Bible, with text in Italian, probably made in Padua near the end of the fourteenth century.[13] A book similar to one of these may have existed in the large Visconti library.

BELBELLO DA PAVIA

In 1912, Pietro Toesca recognized that the illuminator of all but one of the miniatures in the d'Este Bible was the same artist who had completed the Visconti Hours and suggested that he might be the "Belbello" mentioned in correspondence of the Gonzaga family as the author of part of the illumination in a Missal completed by a follower of Andrea Mantegna (Gerolamo da Cremona) for Barbara Gonzaga, Marchioness of Mantua.[14] Among the correspondence is a letter dated March 19, 1462, from Belbello to the Marchioness asking her not to entrust the remainder of the work to another artist but to allow him to complete the illumination even without pay. Earlier, Belbello's work had been more highly esteemed by his Mantuan patrons. In a letter of March 31, 1450, Francesco Gonzaga described to the Bishop of Mantua a ruse by which he had deceived King Alfonso of Aragon: the King had so admired a Missal begun by Belbello for Francesco's brother Gianlucido (who was now dead) that he asked to have it for himself; to avoid complying with the request, Francesco replied that he intended to give the book to the Pope. Belbello's plea to the Marchioness, however, written from Pavia twelve years later, was unsuccessful, and the last documentary reference to him is a letter of October 18, 1462, from Giorgio Valagussa to Bianca Maria Sforza, Filippo Maria's daughter, now Duchess of Milan, recommending Belbello's services to her.

Although the date and place of Belbello's death, like the date of his birth, are unknown, his documented relationship with the Gonzaga family seems to have begun rather late in his career, in 1448, at least fifteen years after his work on the d'Este Bible. Belbello's completion of all but one of the miniatures in the Bible by 1434 has been inferred from a record of payment in that year to Jacopo d'Arezzo for painting the missing miniature. Little else is known of the artist's earlier life. Three miniatures close in style to the Visconti Hours and the Vatican Bible have been attributed to Belbello in a two-volume *Acta Sanctorum* (Milan, Biblioteca Braidense, AE.XIV.19–20), whose first volume is dated 1431. François Avril has recently identified but not yet published as an early work of Belbello the illumination of an *Aeneid* in the Bibliothèque nationale in Paris (lat. 8204).

Most scholars have agreed with Toesca that Belbello's contribution to the Visconti Hours is stylistically earlier than his illumination of the Bible. How much earlier, however, remains uncertain. Inasmuch as the initials F. M. D. M. (probably an abbreviation of Filippo Maria Dux Mediolani) and the ducal coat of arms appear on LF 72, it may be assumed that the portion of the Visconti Hours decorated for Filippo Maria was painted after his accession to the title of Duke in 1412, at the age of twenty, following the assassination of his older brother Giovanni Maria. The portrait of Filippo Maria on LF 57v, though more youthful than his likeness on the Pisanello medal of about 1441, might represent him in his twenties or thirties, and therefore may have been painted at any time between 1412 and the early 1430's.

Although the Duke was a bibliophile, for whom many kinds of manuscripts were written, including treatises on law and medicine and Italian translations of the Roman historians whose works he seems especially to have enjoyed, there is little evidence of an interest in books during the early years of his reign. The absence of manuscripts made for Filippo Maria during this period may be the result of historical circumstances: much of his personal library was lost during the looting of his castle in Milan after his death in 1447. The lack of books may also, however, reflect the Duke's preoccupation between 1412 and 1422, first with securing his succession to the realm, which had been challenged by descendants of his uncle Bernabò, and then with a long but successful attempt to recover his father's territorial possessions, most of which had been lost under the regency of his mother and the incompetent rule of his brother. It seems possible, indeed, that the ducal armorials and the warrior angels holding Visconti shields beside Noah's saving of the animals on LF 72 were intended as reminders of Filippo Maria's role as savior of the Duchy of Milan.

The first dated indication of the Duke's interest in books is the inventory of the Visconti library in Pavia made at his command in January 1426.[15] The earliest surviving dated manuscripts written for him are Italian translations of Suetonius's *Lives of the Caesars*, of 1431, and three Decades of Livy's *Roman History*, whose third Decade bears the date 1432. Both the Suetonius and the Livy were illuminated by the Master of the Vitae Imperatorum. This master and associates also illuminated a Breviary for Marie of Savoy some time after her marriage to Filippo Maria in 1428, and probably before 1435 (Chambéry, Bibliothèque municipale, ms. 4). Belbello also contributed to

27

this Missal, illuminating one gathering (fols. 435v–438) whose historiated initials, borders, and small foliated initials resemble his work in the Visconti Hours. It is possible that the Duke decided to complete his father's Psalter-Hours during a period of intensified interest in book collecting after his inventory of the library and his marriage to Marie.

Much of Belbello's painting in the Visconti Hours clearly stands near the beginning of his stylistic development, which evolves from a compact, detailed, and sometimes gem-like mode to the broader and chromatically more strident vocabulary of the Mantua Missal and some of the single leaves that have been attributed to him as late works. Some of the miniatures in the Vatican Bible are characterized by greater fullness of figure style and compositional groupings than those in the Visconti Hours; nevertheless, similarities of ornament, landscape, color, and modeling suggest that the Hours are not much earlier than the Bible. Lack of homogeneity in the style of the miniatures of the Visconti Hours itself, however, raises questions concerning not only the exact date but also the precise nature of Belbello's contribution. Some of the variations apparent in his part of the manuscript are mentioned in the commentaries to the miniatures. Those which occur near the beginning of the Hours disclose Belbello's intention to conform with the work of the dei Grassi. Elsewhere, differences of quality suggest the intervention of an assistant completing or copying a composition of the master. In still other instances, however, massiveness (sometimes coarseness) of design, occasionally restricted to only parts of a page, remain to be explained either as an aspect of Belbello's own style or as evidence of the participation of associates.[16]

LF 11v, 12, 95v, 99, 101v

LF 29v, 34, 46v

LF 163, 164v

LF 57v, 58, 84v, 85, 128, 166

Plates and Commentaries

Plates and Commentaries

BR 1. *Marriage of Anna and Joachim*

Absent from the canonical New Testament, the Virgin's parents, Anna and Joachim, play an important role in apocryphal accounts of her life. One of these, the early medieval *Gospel of the Nativity of the Virgin*, was incorporated into Jacopo de Voragine's *Golden Legend*, a thirteenth-century compilation of lives of the principal Christian saints which became one of the most popular and influential books of the later Middle Ages.[1] Either the *Nativity Gospel* or the *Legend* may have been the textual source of the narrative of the Virgin in the Visconti Hours. None of the apocrypha, however, emphasizes the episode portrayed on the opening page of the manuscript, the Marriage of Anna and Joachim. Nor is this scene accorded equal prominence in other pictorial cycles; only a few, in fact, even include it. If, however, as suggested in the Introduction, there is a parallel between Joachim and Giangaleazzo, the Visconti miniature may allude to the marriage of the Count and his cousin Caterina. The position of the painting as a kind of frontispiece to the manuscript would then not be surprising.

The gold-rayed sun on the cloth of honor behind the wedding group substantiates an identification between patron and subject. An emblem of the Visconti, this sun is only the first in an inexhaustibly varied and ingenious display of family devices which occurs throughout the manuscript. Nevertheless its place in the opening miniature would be especially appropriate in the context of a Visconti wedding.[2]

The first page of the Visconti Hours is noteworthy for formal as well as biographical reasons. In the upper part of the miniature, especially at the left, paint has been washed away, exposing preparatory drawing in brown ink of women observing and gesticulating from a balcony. The exuberant, generally light tones of the surviving color characterize the painting of Giovannino dei Grassi and his workshop. Also widely prevalent in their part of the manuscript is the red glaze, simulating translucent enamel, applied to the gold leaf which frames the miniature. The *couleur changeant* of the mantle worn by the woman at the left is also symptomatic of the painter's interest in light. Not a scientific representation of the response of color to a specific light, however, the changing color here, which repeats the rose and green worn by Anna, is at least as decorative as it is naturalistic. Exceptional among the veiled and braided heads of Anna's attendants is the classical profile of the woman who wears a coronet, ringlets of hair falling onto her cheek. The delicacy and expressiveness of the hands of the principal participants recur not only on the following folio but on many of the finest miniatures in the book.

BR 1v. *Charity of Anna and Joachim*

Anna and Joachim stand before their palace, novel in representations of this scene which normally show the couple at a table. They distribute gold coins (diminutive replicas of their haloes) and a third object (perhaps a loaf of bread) to the ill, the aged, and the poor. The beggars, some of whose features have been consumed with disease, wear somber, tattered garments which contrast with the colorful gold-edged clothing of Anna and Joachim. The holy couple, however, are now much older than in the preceding miniature. Anna's neck is wrinkled, and Joachim's hair has grown long and gray.

In the borders the Visconti sun alternates with a second emblem of Giangaleazzo, a white dove. Still a third, the most widely used of all Visconti devices, appears in the four corner roundels: a blue viper *(biscia)* swallowing a red man. On this page as elsewhere in the manuscript (for example, BR 1, 18, 23) the reflective quality of gold leaf, used here in haloes, coins, diaper background, frame, and roundels, is enhanced by the gold emulsion pattern strewn in the margins.

BR 2. *Anna and Joachim Pray.*
Expulsion of Joachim from the Temple

Two episodes from the life of Mary's parents are combined in the miniature. In the first the couple pray before an altar, perhaps making the vow that if He grants them a child, they will dedicate it to the service of the Lord. Extremely rare in cycles of Anna and Joachim, this scene may refer in the Visconti manuscript to the vow of Giangaleazzo that he would dedicate to the Virgin any sons born to him.

At the right a priest, having rejected the offering of the childless old man, pushes him out of the temple with one hand, threatening him with the raised fist of the other. Joachim does not hold the doves or lamb customary in this scene. Instead, his outstretched hands overlapping the frame, he is expelled not only from the temple but also from the miniature itself.[3]

The illuminator's fascination with light is evident everywhere on this beautiful though damaged page: in the abundant white of the architecture, in the small strokes of white and deep blue highlighting and shading Joachim's cloak, and above all in the refulgent gold which pervades and unifies the folio.

In the lateral borders a double bar of gold opens into a succession of teardrop forms outlined by numerous smaller gold droplets (from which the red glaze has mostly vanished) and by flickering red penwork which suggests a stylized depiction of light reflected by the gold.[4] In the lower border the golden rays of a Visconti sun pierce through a ring of pink and blue clouds, alternating with a pinwheel of vipers' heads. The pattern created by the sharp teeth of these creatures is reiterated by the extended fingers of their victims.

The skin-like quality of the parchment is apparent in the lower right corner of the folio.

BR 2v. *Joachim in the Wilderness*

On a rocky slope amidst grazing sheep, Joachim sits forlorn, his eyes averted from the herdsmen beneath him. A gesticulating shepherd, wearing one gray and one black shoe, crosses his legs and twists his right arm to hold the staff on which he leans. At his feet a dog lies fast asleep. Seated in the ravine which divides the miniature is a second herdsman, barefoot and muscular, but like Joachim, bearded. His posture too reflects his master's. The only man-made shelter in Joachim's wilderness is the thatch-roofed shed at the peak of the crag behind him.

Emerging from behind a hill, a herd of cows drinks from the stream which flows across the foreground of the miniature, unifying it. Although cows are rare in representations of Joachim among his shepherds, they do occur in at least one earlier North Italian painting.[5] The earlier example does not, however, provide a precedent for the cow snapping at one of the flies on its body. Perhaps aware of the novelty of this detail, the artist painted these insects disproportionately large.

Bright color in Giovannino's world seems to have been a prerogative of the wealthy. The herdsmen, like their animals, are portrayed in brown, gray, black, white, and touches of pink. Large areas of parchment are left unpainted. Within this range of color, however, the painter suggests a remarkable variety of forms and textures.

The second episode of the miniature, which is related to the subject of the facing folio, occurs on a verdant hillside that contrasts with the slope at the upper left. Here an angel brings Joachim the message that Anna will bear a daughter to be named Mary who will herself beget the Son of God. An alert black ram and a cheetah in the right border both seem aware of the importance of the miraculous encounter.[6]

BR 3. *Psalm I*

(MATINS, SUNDAY)

The narrative cycle of Anna and Joachim is interrupted by the introduction of Psalm I. This hymn celebrates all men who have "not walked in the counsel of the ungodly, nor stood in the way of sinners." In the Visconti manuscript, however, it also serves as a kind of gloss on the destiny of Joachim in particular. The Psalm says that the virtuous man "shall be like a tree which is planted near the running waters, which shall bring forth its fruit, in due season." In the preceding miniature Joachim, portrayed beside an abundance of trees planted near running waters, learns from the angel that his wife will not remain barren: "For God indeed punishes not nature, but sin; and therefore, when He closes a womb, it is only that He may later open it more wondrously, and that all may know that what is born thereof is not the fruit of lust, but of the divine munificence" (*Golden Legend*, September 8, Nativity of the Virgin).[7] Compositional similarities between Joachim and the angel on BR 2v and David and the Lord on the facing folio underscore the parallel between the two miniatures. The confrontation of these pages, however, involves still another person, the patron for whom they were painted.

By the late fourteenth century there was a venerable tradition for adorning the first of the Psalms with a portrait of their author, David, playing either a harp or, as in this instance, a psaltery. Giovannino's treatment of the motif is nevertheless spectacularly original. Not even extensive stains obscure the brilliance of the glazed sun against which the scene is depicted. The sun, however, is only the dominant note on a page ablaze with Visconti emblems. Viper shields hang in the niches of the initial and are suspended also from the necks of three damaged lions who rest on its uppermost parapet. Additional *biscia* escutcheons are set within clouds surrounded by angels in the borders, and in two corner roundels they are poised between a pair of Visconti helmets, one surmounted by a viper and the other by a sphere of blue and gold feathers. In the opposite corners, white doves appear in the center of two more suns.

On this first page of text, the illuminator introduces the French motto of Giangaleazzo, *a buon droyt*. Fleur-de-lys in the borders and initial allude to his French title, Comte de Vertus, acquired in 1360 when he married Isabella of Valois and received as part of her dowry the County of Vertus in Champagne.

Just as the position of Psalm I in the manuscript is determined by its function as a commentary on the life of Joachim, the extraordinary display of armorials which accompanies it, emphasizing especially Giangaleazzo's role as the Count of Virtues, identifies him also as the virtuous man honored by the psalmist. Joachim had prayed for a child whom he pledged to the service of the Lord. Giangaleazzo, as indicated in the Introduction, had made a similar vow with regard to his sons. The miniatures on BR 2v and 3 seem to celebrate the fulfillment of both prayers.

The initial on BR 3 is only the first of many in the Visconti Hours which consist mainly of architectural components. Giovannino, however, delights in fusing animate forms into the architecture. Here, for example, diademed angels' heads constitute the upper curve of the B, and its vertical terminates in foliate flourishes. The orange and green of the foliage, especially before the loss at the upper left, would have further connected the facing folios.

BR 18. *Psalm XXI*

The Psalm which begins "O God my God, look upon me: why hast thou forsaken me?" is commonly understood to allude to Christ's Passion. It is so illustrated in the initial where David, wearing a pearled crown and seated on a wooden throne, gestures toward a cloud which supports angels bearing instruments of the Passion. These include column, cross, nails, and the Lord's scarlet vesture. Above the angels hovers the crucified body of Christ, blood seeping from his wounds.

The D *(Deus)* is the first in a series of figural monochromatic initials whose source may be Bohemian illumination.[8] It consists of a portative organist and two wide-eyed creatures whose long arms afford the illuminator an opportunity to indulge a predilection for lavish drapery folds.

A vigorous pod-bearing acanthus scroll shoots out of a patch of glazed gold in the lower left border and twines around two green stalks, curling back on itself to leave an opening at the upper right. Damage to the trilobed forms connected to the foliage has disclosed three stages of glazing: in some the red glaze has adhered; in others it has flaked, exposing gold leaf; and in still others the gold too has disappeared, revealing gray underpaint.

archiquis tuis. preparabis uultum cor
Exaltare domine in uirtute tua. cantabi
mus et psalemus uirtutes tuas

EVS

deus meus r
spice in me. qua
re me dereliq
sti longe a sa

lute mea. uerba delictorum meor
us meus clamabo per diem et non exau
dies. et nocte et non ad insipientiam mi
chi Tu autem in sancto habitas. lau
israel. Inte sperauerunt patres nostri.
sperauerunt et liberasti eos. Ad te clama
uerunt et salui facti sunt. in te sperauerunt

BR 22v. *Annunciation to Anna.*
Meeting at the Golden Gate

With the exception of Psalm CXLII, which is omitted, the Visconti Psalter contains all one hundred and fifty Psalms arranged in numerical sequence. The first one hundred and eight are divided into groups for recitation at Matins on each day of the week beginning with Sunday. Psalm CIX introduces a second cycle, also subdivided, to be recited in the course of the week at Vespers. The daily divisions for Matins are marked by rubrics, sometimes on the preceding page, and by a pair of paintings, one a full-page miniature belonging to the narrative of the Virgin and the other an historiated initial introducing the first Psalm of the group. BR 22v and 23 signal the first ferial subdivision: Matins on Monday.

The angel reveals to Anna the same message he had brought to Joachim and instructs her to meet her husband at the Golden Gate of Jerusalem. In the first scene, the saint's bed is depicted with attention to its most minute details. Her mantle is shaded with delicate strokes of rose. Exquisite refinement characterizes also the embrace of the couple in the second episode. The gate of the city is open, perhaps symbolically, because the Meeting of Anna and Joachim is often understood to signify the conception of the Virgin. A narrow strip of meadow inside the lower frame of the miniature creates a platform which sets the figures into depth. Unnaturalistic on the other hand are the golden sky behind Jerusalem, the pastels, and the innumerable turrets of the city. Equally decorative is the simulated Arabic script in the frame of the miniature.

An interest in both decoration and accurate description distinguishes also the borders of this folio. In the lower margin rabbits (probably intended here to signify fertility) engage in a variety of activities. Two emerge from burrows, and a third licks its paw. A fourth, however, turns to sniff at what appears to be a shimmering reflection of a stylized gold and blue leaf below. Equally improbable are the dwarfed trees set between the rabbits and, despite their roots, the golden trees which grow on either side. From the latter, Visconti shields surmounted by helmets are suspended. Silver in the viper shields and in both visors has tarnished.

BR 23. *Psalm XXVI*

The Psalm which begins "The Lord is my light and my salvation" is traditionally illustrated by David pointing to his eye. Wearing a mantle lined in ermine and a crown set with sapphires and rubies, David worships the Lord, who emerges from a rayed sun and holds a globe in His left hand. Rabbits, a link with the facing page, nibble at the grass on which the king kneels. Four vipers wind around and between two pink bands of the D (*Dominus*), their sinuous movement emphasized by gold stripes on their backs. The blue and gold of the vipers are repeated in the diaper pattern behind the initial. Additional Visconti serpents appear in two secondary initials of the text and in the banners held by winged putti who rise out of acanthus in the borders.

illuminatio mea. 7 salus mea quem time
bo. ✠ ominus protector vite mee. a
quo trepidabo ✠ um appiant super
me noccntes. ut eduiant carnes meas. ✠
✠ ui tribulant me inimici mei. ipsi in
firmati sunt et cecederunt. ✠ i consisti

BR 35v. *Anna and Joachim Give Thanks*

Perhaps designed by the master but painted by a coarser hand, the miniature shows Anna and Joachim giving thanks twice, first in a church and then in their home. The illuminator has either copied from BR 2 or used the same pattern for the ecclesiastical structure in the upper part of the painting. Although the building has been moved higher in the later miniature, it retains the white tiled roof and green balustrade above the altar, as well as the gold scroll, turret, and stepped gable of the pink projection at the right. Adjoining the church in the scenes of thanksgiving is a mauve palace which resembles the orange building in BR 1v, and the bedroom is similar to its predecessor in the *Annunciation to Anna* (BR 22v). The apple tree beside the palace probably alludes to the advent of Mary, the second Eve. It also recalls, however, the words of Psalm I likening the virtuous man to a tree which shall bring forth its fruit in due season.

Peacocks, which adorned the Visconti park in Pavia, also embellish the borders of this folio. In the lower border two of them are disposed with heraldic symmetry among stylized acanthus and oak leaves.[9] Two others sit in gold cages inadequate to accommodate their tails. A fine specimen in the right border presses his crest between blue and gold branches while his counterpart at the left alights behind them. In the upper border a hoopoe perches on a pink bough. Feathery gold emulsion sprays appear in all the margins.

BR 36. *Psalm XXXVIII*

The Psalm begins, "I said: I will take heed to my ways: that I sin not with my tongue." Again following iconographical convention, the illuminator portrays David pointing to his mouth. The Lord responds with a blessing. Like the facing miniature, the scene in the initial is derivative and not so fine as its predecessor, David pointing to his eye on BR 23.

The borders, however, are both novel and ingenious. Beginning at the upper left the artist constructs a gold-leaf frame of Giangaleazzo's motto, *a buon droyt*. The letters are separated by radiant medallions encircled by foliage. One of the roundels in the right border contains fleur-de-lys; three at the left display Visconti suns. A white dove remains visible in the stained medallion at the lower left. Exuberant red penwork enhances both the brilliance and the calligraphic quality of the page. Gold pseudo-script as well as suns and fleur-de-lys adorn the D *(Dixi)* which encloses David.

iam uias meas. ut non delinquam in lin
gua mei. Posui ori meo custodiam. ut
consisterit peccator aduersum me. Ob

BR 48.   *Birth of the Virgin*

Representations of the Birth of the Virgin frequently include details borrowed from the older and more widespread iconography of the Birth of Christ. Derived from the latter are motifs of the midwives, the bath water, and the swaddling of the child. Whereas the Nativity normally occurs in a cave or shed, however (see LF 11), the Birth of Mary takes place in a house. In the Visconti miniature the interior is appointed with unusual splendor. The coffering of Anna's bed repeats the pattern of the ceiling. Wall hanging, counterpane, and curtain consist of richly ornamented fabrics, and all the utensils are golden. Two servants who attend the birth wear almost identical dresses, aprons, and veils; one, who swaddles the Virgin, has unbuttoned and turned up the cuff of her sleeve. Far more elegant is the young woman who washes the saint's hands.

Much in the miniature is designed to suggest depth: the ledge with columns in front of the figures, the canopied bed set at an angle, the barrel-vaulted ceiling, the open door through which one of the women enters. A herringbone pavement set perpendicular to the ledge recalls the miniature of Joachim and Anna giving alms (BR 1v). Quivering black lines around some of the forms (for example, the hands of the midwife and child) also occur in the earlier scene.

Framed but not contained by bands of gold leaf, vigorous falcons and stags embellish the borders. Suns, crowned visors, and shields displaying vipers fill the quatrefoils in the corners.

The stag in the lower margin duplicates in reduced size a drawing on folio 8v of the Bergamo *Taccuino.* The young woman who attends Anna is closely related to a figure on folio 4 of the same sketchbook.

piens incorde suo. non est deus. Corrup
ti sunt et abhominabiles facti sunt inqui
tatibus. non est qui faciat bonum. Deu
de celo prospexit super filios hominum. ut

BR 48v.   *Psalm LII*

Before David and in every way a contrast to him stands the fool who "said in his heart: There is no God." Mouth open, head thrown back on his thick, wrinkled neck, he gesticulates frantically to the dignified king. The rough piece of wood in the crook of his left arm parodies David's scepter.

The D *(Dixit)* is an architectural fantasy of blue and white. Foliage from the meadow within the initial has strayed into the lower curve of the letter where it nourishes numerous rabbits. From an opening at the upper left emerges an arabesque of burnished gold, its tendrils enclosing pink and blue fleur-de-lys as well as glazed, star-like forms. Gold from within the initial extends behind as a foil for a multitude of shields bearing the Visconti *biscia*.

At the bottom of the page appears a catchword, a guide to binding which repeats on the last folio of one gathering of leaves the first word of the next.

BR 60v.   *Presentation of the Virgin in the Temple*

In fulfillment of their vow to dedicate their offspring to the service of the Lord, Anna and Joachim brought Mary to the temple when she was three years old. Placed on the lowest of the steps leading to the altar, the Virgin ascended them unassisted as though she were full-grown. As the family approach the temple in the miniature, Mary, quite small and held by Anna, tenderly touches her mother's cheek. Once within the sanctuary, however, the child, now much larger, turns away from her parents and toward the altar and the priest who extends his arms to receive her. The tip of one golden slipper is visible as she mounts the steep flight of stairs. The front of the altar is golden, but the cloth and triptych upon it are, like the steps, mainly unpainted parchment. Framing the miniature is the motto *a droyt* punctuated by gold emulsion suns. White suns and crowns on blue alternate with burnished gold in the diaper background within the miniature. Gold, blue, red, and green recur in the foliage of the borders. Winged and haloed symbols of the Evangelists appear in the corner roundels.

BR 61.   *Psalm LXVIII*

The miniature within the initial S *(Salvum)* illustrates the opening verse of the Psalm:

> *Save me, O God: for the waters are come in even unto my soul.*
> *I stick fast in the mire of the deep: and there is no sure standing.*
> *I am come into the depth of the sea: and a tempest hath overwhelmed me.*

Waist-deep in turbulent water and battered by a blizzard, David supplicates the Lord. The Deity, who blesses with one hand and holds a scroll in the other, appears together with a heavenly host in a blazing Visconti sun. The sky behind it is free of snow. Two nude putti and two partially draped men clamber amidst the foliage and interlaced gold bands which constitute the initial. A frond of acanthus partially conceals the nudity of the putto at the right, whereas the drapery of the man at the left resembles a leaf as it laps over the frame of the letter. Wrapped around the gold bars, the figures weave them together.

Pod-bearing acanthus in the borders grows out of the initial and reinforces its winding form. Equally sinuous is the more delicate arabesque of gold and red immediately behind the initial.

Through a scribal error the word *Deus* has been omitted from the first horizontal line of text and the word *me* which appears in the vertical line has been repeated instead.

ne quoniam intrauerunt aque ufqȝ
ad animam meam. Jnfixus in limu
p̃ofundi. et non eſt ſubſtantia Deni
an altitudine maris. et tempeſtas demerſit

BR 76. The Virgin Visited by Angels in the Temple

"Joachim and Anna left the child with the other virgins in the Temple, and returned to their home. And Mary advanced in every virtue, and daily was visited by the angels, and enjoyed the vision of God" (Golden Legend). Whereas other representations of the Virgin's life in the temple depict her at work (often weaving) or being fed by an angel, the Visconti miniature shows her held aloft in prayer by twelve angels. This moment in the narrative points ahead to the Annunciation when, according to the apocrypha, Mary did not fear the sight of Gabriel because she had frequently seen the angels and was accustomed to the intensity of celestial light. Iconographically similar to portrayals of the Assumption of the Virgin, the dei Grassi painting is distinguished from them by its indoor setting.

Heavenly light is suggested not only by haloes and rays within the miniature but also by gold in the frame and armorials. Vipers coil around burnished branches at the sides, and Visconti suns gleam in the corners of the page.

adiutori nostro. iubilate deo iacob [S]u
mite psalmum et date tympanum. psalteri
um iocundum cum cythara. [B]ucinate
in comenia tuba. in insigni diei sollempni

BR 76v.   *Psalm LXXX*

Again the miniature illustrates the opening verses of the Psalm:

> *Rejoice to God our helper: sing aloud to the God of Jacob.*
> *Take a psalm, and bring hither the timbrel: the pleasant psaltery with*
> *the harp.*
> *Blow up the trumpet on the new moon, on the noted day of your*
> *solemnity.*

Seated on a draped throne and wearing gold-embroidered clothing, David leads a group of musicians in praising the Lord. The king closely resembles his counterpart on BR 3; even the white pegs of his psaltery are painted with the delicate precision of the earlier miniature. The harp mentioned in the Psalm does not appear; instead one of the participants plays a viol. Family pennants are suspended from the trumpets. Even the doves in the Visconti suns around the initial join in the music, their beaks open wide in song.

As on BR 36, the border decoration is primarily calligraphic. Large gold-leaf letters spelling the motto *a buon droyt* are filled with blue and red on which gold simulated script appears. Between the letters of the motto, pseudo-script and floral motifs are combined in forms which suggest radiating suns. Between the *a* and *b*, however, *a buon droyt* is repeated, and it appears still once more in the initial E (*Exultate*).

BR 90. *Marriage of the Virgin*

Joseph holds the flowering branch upon which the Holy Ghost has alighted in the form of a dove in accordance with the divine prophecy that the Virgin would be espoused to the man who possessed this branch. Disappointed suitors who witness the marriage hold or break the rods which failed to bloom. Mary is attended by seven young women who may represent the seven virgins raised with her in the temple and given to her as companions by the high priest.

Iconographically the *Marriage of the Virgin* resembles the *Marriage of Anna and Joachim* on BR 1. The gestures and clothing of the principal participants resemble those of the earlier miniature. Even the unusual combination of pink and orange worn by the bearded man at the right in BR 1 is repeated, though less subtly, in a corresponding position on BR 90. The enamel-like frame of the opening page is also adapted for the *Marriage of the Virgin* with the addition of simulated pearls at the center of each gold flower.

The marriage of Mary and Joseph takes place in front of three churches, each surmounted by the cylindrical drum characteristic of medieval ecclesiastical architecture in Lombardy. These structures, whose uppermost components exceed the limits of the frame, may have been intended to suggest the venerated basilicas of the Holy Land. They also recall, however, the architectural interests of Giovannino dei Grassi.

Acanthus grows from gold branches in the borders. In the corners golden crowns are encircled by pink and blue clouds and by red, green, and glazed foliage.

domino canticum nouum . quia mirabilia
fecit . **S**aluauit sibi dexteram eius . et
brachium sanctum eius . **N**otum fecit

BR 90v. *Psalm XCVII*

The Psalm invites the worshiper to praise God:

> *Sing ye to the Lord a new canticle: because he hath done wonderful*
> *things....*
> *Make a joyful noise before the Lord our king: let the sea be moved and*
> *the fulness thereof: the world and they that dwell therein.*
> *The rivers shall clap their hands, the mountains shall rejoice together....*

A group of fashionably dressed courtiers sing from a scroll held by the man in the center. This scroll contains not only musical notation but also the letters *dom*, probably the beginning of the word *dominus*. The water and the mountains named in the Psalm appear also in the miniature. In addition, the painter has included other "wonderful things" made by the Lord: a crescent moon at the juncture of the upper and lower halves of the C *(Cantate)* and, opposite it, the sun's rays penetrating pink clouds above an angel who holds a Visconti shield.

With characteristic sensitivity to the decorative unity of the page, the artist provides in the borders a pattern which harmonizes with the scroll and waves in the miniature. Each convolution of the arabesque in the margins terminates in a glazed foliate form resembling a burst of fireworks. Everything in the borders is alive with motion: the leaves, the flowers, and the rippling green stems which attach some of them to the scroll. Even the small lines between the four petals of the gold emulsion flowers, rigid on the reverse of this page, are active here.

Despite staining and loss of glaze, the enamel-like delicacy of the pattern behind the initial survives. Within a blue grid marked by gold at the corners, small white lozenges are set off by a red glazed background.

BR 104v. *The Annunciation*

In a complex architectural setting suggesting numerous spaces, Gabriel confronts the Virgin, separated from her by a low wall. Mary kneels beneath a canopy of honor set at an angle to reveal the space behind it. A pillow lies at her feet. Inscribed in the book on the altar are two words of her reply to the angelic salutation, *Ecce ancilla....* ("Behold the handmaiden of the Lord, be it done to me according to thy word." [Luke I:38]). Emanating from God the Father, the dove of the Holy Spirit descends on rays of light toward the Virgin. Higher in the painting, the Child himself, nude and cross-nimbed, follows.[10] The lower ranks of the heavenly host are depicted in the luminous rose-tinted white of Gabriel's raiment and in the blue of Mary's mantle; fiery red is reserved for the angels closest to God. In the borders, glittering stem-like bands twine and open into a variety of shapes which incorporate Visconti suns, vipers, and fleur-de-lys.

The cycle of the Virgin in the Visconti Psalter culminates with the Annunciation. The narrative of her life continues in Landau–Finaly 22 where, however, it illustrates the Hours of the Virgin.

BR 105. *Psalm CIX*

Representations of the Trinity frequently illustrate the opening verse of the Psalm, "The Lord said to my Lord: Sit thou at my right hand. . . ." Within the D *(Dixit)* Father and Son, clothed identically and both bearded, cross-nimbed, and holding books, sit beside one another on a large throne surrounded by angels. The dove of the Holy Spirit, however, appears not in the miniature but rather in the upper border. Here, complementing the portrait of the Count of Virtues below, the bird refers not only to the Holy Ghost but also to the emblem of Giangaleazzo previously depicted on BR 1v and 3. Likewise, the celestial rays around the dove and behind the initial suggest the Visconti sun. Pink-banded falcons perched on stylized oaks at the sides of the page constitute still another personal allusion, in this instance to the Count's passion for hunting.

Like the beginning of Psalm I (BR 3) which introduces the cycle for Matins, the opening Psalm of the Vespers cycle is distinguished by extraordinary embellishment not only of its initial but also of the following letters. The large display script of gold leaf and red is further adorned with pink and blue flowers. The Vespers page resembles BR 3 also in its position opposite the representation of an angelic annunciation of a child to be born. Whereas on the earlier page the motto and devices of Giangaleazzo were extraordinarily prominent, on BR 105 the Count himself, in three-quarter profile, smiles at the miracle depicted on the facing folio. This representation of Giangaleazzo is the first of three surviving in the manuscript (two others appear on BR 115 and 128). An offset on BR 150 indicates that the folio originally opposite and now missing also included a portrait of the Count in its lower margin. (See also the commentary for BR 148v.)

The bust of Giangaleazzo, set within a trefoil, is recessed into depth by an inner frame which echoes the scalloping around the angels in the initial as well as the pattern in the quatrefoils on the facing folio. Glazed gold leaf also relates the portrait both to the initial and to the letters which follow. The decorative unity of the page is further enhanced by vine-encircled oaks in the borders which reiterate the motif of meandering tendrils in the outline of the D.

BR 108v.   *Psalm CXIV*

The illustration of Ferial Psalters commonly ends with the miniature for Psalm CIX at the opening of the Vespers cycle. The exceptionally rich Visconti Psalter, however, includes miniatures at the beginning of each feria for Vespers as well as Matins. Hence, Psalm CXIV, which introduces the recitation for Vespers on Monday but is rarely illustrated, is here illuminated with one of the finest miniatures in the book. All the letters of the opening words of the Psalm are accorded the special prominence found elsewhere in the Psalter only at Matins and Vespers for Sunday (BR 3 and 105). In all three folios the initial is set against a rayed sun. On 108v, moreover, a multitude of diminutive suns are strewn in the borders.

Within the D *(Dilexi)* David prays, illustrating the opening verse of the Psalm, "I have loved, because the Lord will hear the voice of my prayer." The psalmist's long white hair falls onto a white mantle delicately shaded in blue. Beside him lie his crown and a pillow. An angular bench defines the space in which he kneels. The Lord's head emerges from an aureole of green clouds which harmonize with the scroll-patterned cloth upon the bench. Beyond it a blue and gold lattice contains tiny white squares dotted with even smaller circles. In outline the D resembles the architectural-foliate forms of BR 3, 48v, and 150v. On parapets to either side, putti simultaneously enhance the liveliness of the design and underscore the three-dimensional structure of the initial. Some of these creatures are bald as well as nude; two at the left, however, pull tufts of one another's hair. Another putto above prepares to scramble up a ladder to a barred window, while his companion aims a gold, rounded dart into a pink cloud.

In the upper border, winged putti provide music for David's prayer. At the sides, two of the Cardinal Virtues adopted as emblems by the Comte de Vertus hold helmets surmounted by Visconti crests: the viper and a sphere of feathers (see also BR 3, 22v, 48, 128). Justice, her headdress suggested by a pouf of brown dots, grasps a sword. Its silver blade, now tarnished, together with the visors above and the fish below, must originally have been a prominent metallic accompaniment to the gold on the page. At the right Temperance dilutes one liquid with another from a second golden vessel.

The painting in the lower border illustrates the last verse of the Psalm, "I will please the Lord in the land of the living." The landscape (its salmon tint a lighter restatement of the color in the Virtues' gowns) is alive with trees, fish, birds, rabbits, and a variety of human dwellings. Of the eight birds who inhabit the scene the parakeet is the largest; liveliest, however, is the stork who has alighted on the tower of the castle at the right. Neck arched and beak agape, he calls in the direction of the initial above.

BR 111. *Psalm CXVIII:1*

The longest Psalm is CXVIII, which contains twenty-two sections of eight verses each, originally corresponding to the letters of the Hebrew alphabet. It is divided in the Visconti manuscript for recitation at four of the Canonical Hours and illustrated with a miniature at each. At Prime, David, wearing a pearl-studded crown, addresses a group of men within the initial B *(Beati)*. The blue mantle of the man in the foreground is highlighted with fine strokes of white and falls gracefully from his left arm. The figures stand on a green plane which darkens as it recedes, suggesting depth even within a small space. Divided strokes in the outline of the initial are linked by lozenges, two of which enclose damaged Visconti shields. Separating the first lines of the Psalm are glazed gold and emulsion patterns, and the entire text is framed by gold edging and foliage. Glittering movement continues in the borders where petals and entire flowers curl and bend into space, imparting both vitality and depth to the pattern.

meus es tu et exaltabo te. Confitebor ti
bi quoniam exaudisti me. et factus es mi
chi insalutem. Confitemini domino
quoniam bonus. quoniam insecula mi
sericordia eius. Ad primam psalmus cxviii.

Eati immacula
ti invia. q am
bulant inlege
domini. Bea
ti qui scrutant
testimonia eius. intoto corde exquirunt
eum. Non enim qui operantur iniqui
tatem. inviis eius ambulauerunt. Tu
mandasti mandata tua. custodiri nimis.
Utinam dirigantur vie mee. ad custodien

me inuenebis tuus. Uiam uniquitatis a
moue a me. 7 de lege tua miserere mei. Uia
ueritatis elegi. iudicia tua non sum oblitus.
Adhesit testimonys tuis domine noli
me confundere. Uiam mandatorum tuo
rum. cucurri cum dilatasti cor meum.
Usq ad terciam Psalmus:

Legem pone
michi domi
ne uiam iu
stificationum
tuarum. 7 ex
quiram eam
semper. Da michi intellectum 7 scruta

BR 112v. *Psalm CXVIII: 33*

David prays, "Set before me for a law the way of thy justifications, O Lord." In response the Almighty extends an open book toward him. Combining a variety of reds, orange, and pink, the illuminator achieves an unusual harmony of color. Red glaze pervades all parts of the page. The upright of the L *(Legem)* terminates in flourishes of acanthus which also dominates the borders. Its robust foliage winds about oaks which open to admit Giangaleazzo's motto, *a droyt*. In the lower margin a rabbit nestles between two clusters of leaves. The delicate gold "tree" in the upper border evokes the *joyaux* produced by goldsmiths contemporary with Giovannino.

A catchword appears at the bottom of the folio because, like BR 48v, it concludes a gathering.

BR 115.   *Psalm CXVIII:81*

The miniature is unrubricated. Space has been left for a rubric, however, and it probably was intended to designate the portion of Psalm CXVIII to be recited at Sext. Why Giangaleazzo's portrait appears in the midst of this Psalm is not apparent. It is nevertheless the most imposing representation of him in the manuscript. His profile discloses the sloping brow, receding hairline, full lips, and double-pointed beard depicted also in the three-quarter views on BR 105 and 128. It is, however, larger than the other portraits and given additional prominence by the ring of clouds and the sunburst which frame it. At either side of the Count are his hunting dogs and their quarry, the latter represented in a striking variety of postures. Trees similar to those on BR 22v and 105 emerge from precipitous hills. Although their foliage and golden bark are more decorative than naturalistic, the artist conspicuously includes their roots as well as those of the vines which grow around them. Trumpet-shaped blossoms on the winding tendrils complement the flowers on the hills and meadow below.

The miniature itself is one of the most exquisitely painted and best preserved in the book. David sits on a faldstool beneath an architectural canopy supported by slender columns. Its green vaults and tessellated pavement, together with a patterned red cloth hung against gold, provide a sumptuous setting for the king. His scarlet robe and ermine-lined mantle are elegantly draped. Amidst this splendor the Lord himself, holding a golden orb, is almost insignificant.

The D *(Defecit)* consists of a twisted ribbon adorned with fleur-de-lys. It terminates in an acanthus pod about to open. Behind it a golden arabesque and its blue ground reiterate the colors of the pattern behind the Count. Four shields with vipers and a motto in the upper border complete the array of his devices.

ego autem exercebor in mandatis tuis. Co
nertantur michi timentes te. et qui nouerut
testimonia tua. Fiat cor meum immacu
latum. in iustificationibus tuis ut non co
fundar.

Efecit in
Salutari i
tuo. ani
ma mea
7 in verbu
tuum sup

speram. Defecerunt oculi mei in eloq
uium tuum. dicendo quando consolaberis
me. Quia factus sum sicut uter in pru

testimonia tua . ideo scrutata est aia mea.
eclaratio sermonum tuorum illumi
nat . 7 intellectum dat parvulis . s
meum aperui 7 atraxi spiritum . quia ma
data tua desiderabam . spice in me 7

BR 117v.   *Psalm CXVIII:129*

The M (*Mirabilia*) consists of a rim of blue clouds and angels' heads and a central stroke of three figures and a ladder. A winged angel assists a half-naked man in his ascent to heaven while a second man kneels to adore the Deity. The Lord appears in full length within a mandorla. He is cross-nimbed and holds an orb and scepter. In the other half of the initial, David occupies a Gothic throne. The borders, dominated by gold and dense blue, are more rigid than most of those which precede.

q̄ luna per noctem **D**ominus custo
dit te ab omni malo. custodiat animam tua
dominus **D**ominus custodiat introy
tum tuum. et exitum tuum. exhoc nunc
usq̄ insecalum.

Feria .iij. ad uesperum. Psalmus dauid

que

BR 120v. *Psalm CXXI*

The miniature exemplifies the influence of court life on medieval illustration of religious texts. The Psalm begins, "I rejoiced at the things that were said to me: We shall go into the house of the Lord." The Lord, however, is absent from the painting, and the rejoicing is distinctly secular. Much younger than in the foregoing miniatures (his brow unfurrowed, his hair untouched by white), David listens to courtiers play a viol, a psaltery, and a portative organ. Two hunting dogs accompany the king. Within the L (*Letatus*) a young couple play chess in a gracefully draped pavilion. Although Cardinal Virtues appear in the initial as emblems of Giangaleazzo, they are elegant ladies, at home in a courtly environment. Temperance repeats the action of BR 108v. Her companion, Fortitude, holds a club and a shield embossed with a lion's head. The figures in the initial are modeled with exceptionally delicate strokes of blue and white pigment.

The rectangular frame glows with burnished and glazed gold and is quickened by red, gray, and blue penwork. Angular geometric patterns of the borders are reflected by marquetry in David's throne and by the chessboard. The Count's French motto finds its counterpart in the fleur-de-lys of the miniature.

A rubric designates the group of Psalms to be recited at Vespers on the third feria (Tuesday). The catchword identifies BR 120v as the last folio in a gathering.

facere cum eis. Magnificauit dominus
facere nobiscum. facti sumus letantes.
Conuertere domine captiuitatem no
stram. sicut torrens in austro. Qui se
minant in lacrimis. in exultatione metet.
Euntes ibant et flebant. mittentes se
mina sua. Uenientes autem venient
cum exultatione. portantes manipulos
suos. Feria quarta ad uesperum psalmus

BR 122v. *Psalm CXXVI*

"Unless the Lord build the house, they labour in vain that build it." The illuminator's illustration of this Psalm discloses familiarity with the accoutrements and practices of the building trade. Scaffolds, ladder, pulley, pick, trowel, bricks, and mortar are used by workmen whose agility and vigor surpass their physical robustness. Their buildings too are both delicate and sturdy. David himself oversees construction, and bands of angels in the borders give it divine sanction. At the same time they display banderoles bearing the motto of Giangaleazzo. The pinks, red, blue, and green of these heavenly apparitions echo the principal colors of the miniature and of the beautiful flourishes which terminate the N *(Nisi)*.

mine dauid. et omnis manfuetudinis
cius. [S]icut iurauit domino. uotum
uouit deo iacob. [S]i introicro intaber
naculum domus mcc. si ascendero in lec
tum strati mci. [S]i dedero sompnium

BR 124v. *Psalm CXXXI*

"O Lord, remember David, and all his meekness." David resembles the kneeling king on BR 108v, and the full-length Deity within a mandorla is similar to the Lord on BR 117v. Both figures, however, are painted more coarsely than their predecessors. Nothing, on the other hand, is inferior in the design of the folio and the painting of its borders. Irradiated by a shower of gold stars and droplets, two oaks and a crenellated rabbit hutch frame the miniature. Energetic vines encircle the trees, bearing red grapes on one side and golden clusters on the other. The rhythm of the stems is enhanced by their golden tendrils and by arabesques around the Visconti shield in the upper margin. In the lower border a grazing stag has mysteriously slipped his antlers through an improbably small opening in a gold picket fence. Tall, liliate flowers screening the rabbits' pen harmonize with floral patterns in the M *(Memento)* and in the enamel-like design behind it.

BR 128. *Psalm CXXXVII*

The initial introduces the verse, "I will praise thee, O Lord, with my whole heart." In the miniature the illuminator strives to suggest space, especially by depicting only parts of objects. David kneels in a meadow enclosed by wickets and a lattice wall. Beyond the enclosure the lower portion of a building is indicated, and the Deity seems to emerge between it and the initial. Partially visible behind David are his throne, a cloth hanging which turns a corner, and a canopy. Even his mantle is truncated. The C itself *(Confitebor)* is modeled to suggest depth, and the daisies which adorn it are shown from various points of view.

The borders are rich in armorials including the final portrait of Giangaleazzo that survives in the manuscript (see also BR 105, 115). The Count and his dove appear within blazing suns. Equally radiant mandorlas contain Visconti helmets and shields.

tribuet tibi retributionem tuam quam
retribuisti nobis. ⟨B⟩ eatus qui tene
bit. ⟨et⟩ allidet paruulos suos ad petram.
⟨G⟩loria patri et filio. et spiritui sancto
⟨S⟩icut erat in principio et nunc et semp.
et in secula seculorum. Amen.

Feria. VI. Ad uesperum. psalmus. cll.

BR 132. *Psalm CXLIII*

"Blessed *be* the Lord my God, who teacheth my hands to fight, and my fingers to war." The Psalm is often illustrated by David's encounter with Goliath (1 Kings 17:49–51). Prematurely crowned in the Visconti miniature, the victorious youth assumes an elegant pose, his left thumb hooked into his cincture. He is, however, prepared to hurl a second stone from the sling behind his head. The first has already struck its target: the swarthy, dark-eyed giant lies fallen, blood streaming from his forehead, his right hand raised in self-defence, his enormous club useless beside him. The event occurs in a hilly landscape, delicately graded in color from green to salmon-pink to bluish white.

Flowers are prominent in the design of the B *(Benedictus)* as in other initials near the end of the Psalter (BR 122v, 124v, 128, 148v, 151). On BR 132 they also frame the borders of the folio. The flowers as well as the "script"-filled bars in the margins, however, are more rigid and less interesting than their counterparts elsewhere in the book.

enevictas

dominus deus meus . qui docet manus
meas ad prelium . 7 digitos meos ad bellu.
Misericordia mea et refugium meu . su

BR 136. *Psalm CXLVIII*

The miniature introduces the last three Psalms, all of them invitations to praise God. They are rubricated on BR 135v for recitation at Lauds. The Visconti miniature follows the convention of depicting creations of the Lord, which are exhorted to glorify Him:

> Praise ye the Lord from the heavens: praise ye him in the high places.
> Praise ye him, all his angels: praise ye him, all his hosts.
> Praise ye him, O sun and moon: praise him, all ye stars and light.
> Praise him, ye heavens of heavens: and let all the waters that are above the heavens praise the name of the Lord.
> For he spoke, and they were made: he commanded, and they were created.
> He hath established them forever, and for ages of ages: he hath made a decree, and it shall not pass away.
> Praise the Lord from the earth, ye dragons, and all ye deeps:
> Fire, hail, snow, ice, stormy winds, which fulfil his word:
> Mountains and all hills, fruitful trees and all cedars:
> Beasts and all cattle: serpents and feathered fowls:
> Kings of the earth and all people: princes and all judges of the earth:
> Young men and maidens: let the old with the younger, praise the name of the Lord: for his name alone is exalted.
> The praise of him is above heaven and earth: and he hath exalted the horn of his people.
> A hymn to all his saints: to the children of Israel, a people approaching to him. Alleluia.

Angels, sun, moon, stars, and light; heavens, waters, hills, and trees; beasts, serpents, and feathered fowls; kings of the earth and princes; young and old—all are represented in the miniature. So, too, are snow and stormy winds, the latter ingeniously indicated by whirling leaves.

One of the most inventive initials in the manuscript, the L *(Laudate)* consists of two serpents (or one twin-headed monster) and a lion who holds a Visconti pennant and looks with justified foreboding in the direction of his tail. A blossom set off by Visconti rays separates the reptile heads. Behind the initial, a diaper pattern of gold and green is enlivened by minute white crowns.

Like others in the latter part of the Psalter (see, for example, BR 117v, 132, 147v) the design of the borders is comparatively heavy. Visconti suns, acanthus, and viper shields in the margins reinforce the motifs and colors of the miniature.

num dīcelis. laudate eum in excelsis. La
udate eum omnes angeli eius. laudate eu
omnes uirtutes eius. Laudate eum sol

BR 145. *The Three Hebrews in the Fiery Furnace*

Canticles (songs or prayers, other than Psalms, derived from the Bible) frequently follow the Psalms in Psalters. During the course of the week, seven Old Testament canticles were recited, at Lauds. All seven appear in the Visconti manuscript (BR 137v–146), but only the last, the Canticle of the Three Hebrews, is illustrated. The third chapter of the Prophecy of Daniel recounts the refusal of three companions of the prophet—Misach, Sidrach, and Abdenago—to worship a golden statue erected by King Nebuchadnezzar. Cast by the Babylonian into a furnace, the Hebrews are safely delivered from it by the Lord.

The miniature shows a polygonal, buttressed furnace, red-hot from the flames which leap out of its numerous apertures. Within are the Hebrews, their prayers unimpeded by the blaze. Above the furnace their names are inscribed on a scroll irradiated by burnished gold leaf. The B (*Benedicite*) is under construction by four putti, who knot together a series of staves and boughs which they then drape with pink cloth. Fleur-de-lys grow out of the branch at the upper left, and another Visconti emblem, the sun, appears in quatrefoils set into the tessellated pattern behind the initial.

The borders combine additional armorials of Giangaleazzo with representations of scenes related to the miniature. In the upper margin a tarnished shield is flanked by scroll-entwined branches. The inscription on these banderoles is almost entirely effaced, but the words *a droyt* are still legible (with the aid of a magnifying glass) at the left. Beneath the text, a dog similar to one of those on BR 120v is framed by an ellipse of oak leaves and glazed acorns illumined by omnipresent Visconti rays.

To the left of the miniature, Moses receives the tablets of the law. Inscribed on the tablets are two commandments. The first, *Non adorabis deos alienos*, conflates the injunctions given to Moses not to have strange gods nor to adore graven images. It was, of course, in obedience to these prohibitions that the Three Hebrews declined to worship Nebuchadnezzar's idol. The second commandment in the painting is the eighth given to Moses, *Non furtum faties*.

Complementing the gift of the Old Law, the New Dispensation is granted at the right. Standing on a bank high above the Jordan, St. John baptizes the cross-nimbed Savior. The Spirit of God descends as a dove upon Christ, and the scroll beneath it bears the words of God the Father in Matthew 3:17, *Hic est filius meus dilectus in quo m. . . .* ("This is my beloved Son, in whom I am well pleased.") The illuminator stresses parallels between the scenes at left and right: similar plants support the figures, and identical Deities emerge from blue clouds and golden rays on either side. Christ blesses the Hebrews in the furnace, as though illustrating his words,

> *Do not think that I have come to destroy the Law or the Prophets.*
> *I have not come to destroy, but to fulfill. (Matthew 5:17)*

omnia opera domini domino. laudate
et super eraltate eum in seeula. [B]ene
dicite angeli domini domino. benedicite

dominus deus israel. quia uisitauit et fecit
redemptionem plebis sue. Et erexit
cornu salutis innobis. indomo dauid pue

BR 146v. *Zacharias*

In addition to the seven Old Testament canticles, Psalters normally include three derived from the Gospel of Luke. Originally the Visconti manuscript contained all three Evangelical canticles, and it seems probable that each was illuminated. Only the miniatures of the first two survive, however (see also the commentary for BR 148v). The first of these introduces the canticle sung by Zacharias at the birth of his son John the Baptist (Luke 1:68–79). The song, which prophesies salvation through a savior, is sometimes adorned with representations of the Annunciation to Zacharias or the Naming of the Baptist. The canticle in the Visconti Psalter belongs to a third group, illustrated by Zacharias prophesying.

Wearing the turban-like cap which often designates prophets in medieval portrayals, Zacharias holds a scroll which, unlike those in the preceding miniature, appears never to have borne an inscription. Its function is largely decorative: together with the body of Zacharias himself it reinforces the rhythm of the initial. This movement extends out of the initial into the borders where a foliate scroll is given exceptional vitality by the pods and flowers which grow out of it. Characteristically, the illuminator does not close the border but prefers to leave breathing space at left and right between two sections of arabesque.

Like the initials on BR 61 (also framed by a similar arabesque), 111, and 132, the B *(Benedictus)* consists of separate strands intricately woven together. Its spaces incorporate fleur-de-lys and red glaze patterned with gold.

anima mea dominum. Et exaltauit
spiritus meus. in deo salutari meo. Qui
respexit humilitatem ancelle sue. ecce ei
ex hoc beatam me dicent. omnes genera

BR 147v.   The Virgin with St. John and St. Elizabeth

The miniature introduces the *Magnificat*, a prayer recited by the Virgin on the occasion of her visit to Elizabeth before the birth of their children (Luke 1:46–55). Frequently this canticle is illustrated by the Visitation, a scene which occurs in the Visconti prayerbook immediately preceding the Hours of the Virgin (LF 10v). For the Psalter, however, the illuminator chose a moment after the birth of the Baptist. He is shown as an infant (proleptically wearing his shirt of camel's hair) in the firm, maternal grasp of the woman at the right. She, however, appears to be not his mother but rather the Virgin, traditionally veiled by a blue mantle (see also LF 10v). The more modishly dressed woman who holds a book bearing a simulated inscription probably represents St. Elizabeth. The painting seems to reflect Italian literature of the thirteenth and fourteenth centuries which popularized an apocryphal account of Mary's sojourn with her cousin before and after the Baptist's birth. The *Meditations on the Life of Christ*, for example, recounts the care Mary gave to Elizabeth's child:

> When her time had come Elizabeth gave birth to the son whom our Lady lifted from the ground and diligently cared for as was necessary. . . . She played with him, gaily embracing and kissing him with joy. . . . No one ever had a nurse or governess like this. . . .[11]

Like his hair shirt, the pointing gesture is an attribute of the Precursor. The Savior to whom he normally points, however, is not represented in the miniature.

In the M (*Magnificat*) four young women play catch. They are sheltered by acanthus which grows tube-like out of a rabbit-populated terrain.

The borders are heavier than those which precede. A dense mass of flowers, fruit, and foliage is painted on a wide gold band which almost fills the margins. Much of the pigment has flaked, exposing parchment as well as gray underpaint. Red penwork at the top of the page has been trimmed.

mus. te dominum confitemur: **A** e
eternum patrem. omnis terra ueneratur.
Tibi omnes angeli. tibi celi et uniuer

BR 148v. *Saints Ambrose and Augustine*

The *Te Deum*, a hymn which frequently accompanies the canticles at the end of Psalters, was long believed to have been composed by Saints Ambrose and Augustine at the latter's baptism. The saints are depicted here beneath the arms of the T. Both are identified as bishops by their mitres and croziers. Ambrose holds a whip, his attribute as a scourge of heretics. St. Augustine, according to tradition, wears black monastic garb beneath his cope.

At the end of the *Te Deum* on BR 149v, the following rubric appears: *Canticum Simeonis pphete.* The leaf originally facing this folio has been cut out of the manuscript. It must have contained the third Evangelical canticle, *Nunc dimittis*, recited by Simeon at the Presentation of Christ in the Temple (Luke 2:29–32). It was perhaps illustrated conventionally by a portrayal of the Presentation within the initial N. The verso of the missing folio probably contained the beginning of the hymn to the Trinity, *Gloria in excelsis*, the end of which appears on BR 150. The opening of this hymn may have been adorned by a representation of the Trinity. An offset on BR 150 discloses the presence of falcons at the sides and a portrait in the lower border of the missing leaf. Falcons and a portrait of Giangaleazzo appear in the same positions on BR 105 which also represents the Trinity.

BR 150v. *Sermon on the Mount*

Like canticles and hymns, the *Pater Noster* and creeds are often included in Psalters. The *Pater Noster* begins here with a representation of Christ instructing his disciples in the prayer (Matthew 6:9–13).

As the Apostles look up to Christ in the initial, figures in the borders gaze at manifestations of his divinity. At the left the Tiburtine Sibyl indicates to the Emperor Augustus the apparition of the Virgin and Child in the sun (the Ara Coeli). [12] The Emperor, wreathed in leaves and wearing a splendid though damaged mantle, worships the child who will be greater than he. The legend of the Ara Coeli is recounted by Jacopo de Voragine in the reading for December 25 of the *Golden Legend*. The same chapter includes an account of another astronomical phenomenon which likewise occurred on the day of the Nativity: "The same day, certain Magi were praying on a mountain, and saw a star appear which had the form of a fair child, bearing over his head a cross of fire." The second miracle is portrayed in the right border of BR 150v. [13]

BR 151. *Apostles*

Seated in a circle within the initial, twelve Apostles recite their Creed. The opening verse is attributed by the rubric to Peter; the second is rubricated for Andrew.

Strange winged creatures inhabit the borders amidst an arabesque of burnished gold and flowers. In the upper margin, butterflies flit through the scroll. An offset of the star seen by the Magi appears at the upper left.

ter qui es incelis. Sanctifi
cetur nomen tuum. Adue
niat regnum tuum. Fiat
uoluntas tua. Sicut ince
lo et interra. Panem nrm
cottidianum da nobis hodie.
Et dimitte nobis debita no
stra. Sicut et nos dimittim

debitoribus nris. Et ne nos in du
cas intemptationem. Sed libera nos
amalo. Amen. Symbolu aplorum.

um patrem omnipotentem creatorem
celi et terre. Andreas. Et in iħesu
xpm filium eius unicum dominum nrm.

LF 1.   *A Bishop Addresses the Faithful*

The first pages of Landau–Finaly 22 continue the Psalter begun in Banco Rari 397. Folio 1 introduces the Athanasian Creed. Ascribed incorrectly by tradition to Athanasias, Bishop of Alexandria, the prayer is illustrated by a representation of a bishop addressing his congregation. Mitred and holding a white crozier, he stands before an altar in the raised apse of a church. The front of the altar is partially glazed gold. Its top is draped with a patterned cloth on which a second, unadorned cloth covers the Host. Other parts of the miniature are portrayed with similar attention to detail. A minute representation of the Madonna and Child appears in the triangular pediment of the church. The clothing of the bishop's audience is carefully patterned and trimmed. Two of his listeners seem to exchange a word during his sermon.

Like their predecessors in the *Magnificat* (BR 147v) the figures in the Q (*Quicunque*) are set into fronds of acanthus. Unlike the women in the earlier miniature, however, these are servants. One holds a goose, the other rides a donkey, and both carry baskets on their heads. The stem of the initial drifts across the text into the border of the folio.

The wide floral borders stiffly edged in red, the blue monochromatic initial, the diaper pattern, and even the subject of the miniature resemble their counterparts on BR 136. Novel, however, is the punched and squared gold leaf behind the initial on LF 1. In each compartment, a four-petaled flower is painted in gold emulsion against the burnished ground. This is a favorite design of Belbello da Pavia, the second major illuminator of the Visconti Hours. It recurs frequently in his part of the manuscript (for example, LF 90v, 99, 102).

ult saluus esse. ante omnia opus est ut
teneat catholicam fidem. Quam nisi qs
qs integram inuiolatamqs suauerit. abs

LF 4v.   *The Lord in Majesty with Saints and Angels*

In the Visconti manuscript, as in most liturgical Psalters, litanies of the saints follow the canticles, hymns, and creeds. Saints and angels petitioned to intercede with the Lord are ranged in hieratical order within the initial K *(Kyrie)*. At the top, the Diety appears within a mandorla. He blesses with His right hand, and in His left holds an open book whose golden hasp falls onto His lap. To either side are the Virgin, St. John, and angels. In the lower segment of the initial are other saints, including two deacons in the second row from the bottom (probably Lawrence and Stephen). The virgins, invoked last, are in the lowest rank. Identifiable by their attributes are Mary Magdalen with long hair and a pyxis, Catherine with her wheel beside her, Margaret holding a dragon, and Lucy with a burning lamp.

Not surprisingly, the illuminator introduces Visconti emblems into the celestial court. Radiating suns embellish the initial, and the borders are adorned with the *biscia* in various forms.

LF 10v. *Visitation*

At the conclusion of the litanies and opposite the beginning of the Hours of the Virgin is a miniature of the Visitation. Returning to the narrative of the Virgin, the illuminator returns also to the segmented gold frames used for earlier episodes of her life in Banco Rari 397. Where gold leaf has flaked in this part of the manuscript, however, red rather than gray underpaint is visible.

Elizabeth kneels to welcome her cousin. The drapery of both women is heavier than in preceding miniatures, and the landscape less delicate. In the borders, elements of the design evoke earlier pages (for instance, BR 2v, 36). They are, however, differently and inconsistently integrated. Penwork appears in the left and lower margins but not in the others. The colors too, especially some of the blues, are foreign to what precedes.

LF 11. *The Nativity*

(HOURS OF THE VIRGIN. MATINS)

One of the richest folios in the manuscript, LF 11 offers a miniature by the workshop of Giovannino and borders decorated a generation later by Belbello da Pavia, in the second major campaign of illumination. The text designated by the rubric as the Hours of the Virgin according to the Use of Rome is introduced at Matins by the Nativity. Mary proffers the partially swaddled child to a midwife who extends long arms to receive him. A second midwife pours bath water and tests its temperature, while Joseph simultaneously warms additional swaddling cloth and the sole of one of his feet. The ox and ass kneel to worship the child.[14] One corner of the thatched shed is supported by a pink pillar which may allude to the column against which the Virgin is said to have stood at the moment of Christ's birth.[15] The foreground of the painting is warmed by a yellow glow which seems to emanate from the radiant child.[16] Patches of green and gray beyond the infant may represent areas unillumined by divine light.

With the exception of the cross-nimbed head of God the Father, the borders appear to have been painted entirely by Belbello. His debut in the manuscript is spectacularly unhesitant. On a platform of hills which sweep from the lower margin into the sides of the page, four shepherds learn of the Nativity; a fifth dozes, unaware of the event. The full-cheeked, swarthy young shepherds are types much favored by Belbello. So too is their elderly, weatherbeaten companion whose jutting beard emphasizes the tilt of his head. The mist of fine white hatching which lights the shepherds' clothing is characteristic of the illuminator. Distinctive also are the yellow foliage and small white flowers strewn on the hills, and the dense clusters of fruit-bearing trees behind them. Arabesques of punched gold ivy, introduced on this folio, recur frequently on subsequent pages of the manuscript. They enclose prominently outlined, voluminous blossoms whose colors repeat those of the angels' wings and raiment.

LF 11v and 12.   *Celestial Court and Fall of the Rebel Angels*

This diptych represents, on the left, the Lord in Majesty and, on the right, the punishment of the rebel angels. The radiant Deity blesses with His right hand and holds keys in His left.[17] He is surrounded within the D *(Domine)* by worshiping angels who extend beyond the initial as a kind of feathered aureole. The celestial court also includes Virtues. The three Theological Virtues are disposed in a triangle: Faith in the upper margin, part of her crown and chalice lost through trimming; Hope, winged and holding an anchor; and Charity bearing a sheaf of grain. Beneath architectural canopies to either side of the Deity are two of the four Cardinal Virtues: Prudence holds calipers and a mirror which reflects one of her three faces, and Justice balances a pair of gold scales. Their sisters appear in the upper corners of the folio: Fortitude armed with a mace and shield, a lionskin draped over her head; and Temperance who, though damaged, appears to hold a vessel in each of her hands (see also BR 120v). The veiled woman in the lower margin may represent Humility, often regarded as the root of all other Virtues.

Within the D *(Deus)* on the facing folio, four militant angels expel Lucifer from heaven. Some of the red trefoil arches surrounding the central group enclose angels' heads painted in gold against blue. Others, however, are empty, perhaps vacated by the fallen creatures who spill onto burnished gold behind the initial and into the borders, where they are pursued by elegant tormentors.

The subjects depicted on LF 11v and 12 are rare in Books of Hours. They may be related to a legendary debate among the Virtues widely circulated through its appearance as the introduction to the account of man's redemption in the *Meditations on the Life of Christ*.[18] Five thousand years after original sin, the angels implore the Deity to allow man to rise from misery to his heavenly home. They remind the Lord that He created man in His own image in reparation for the fall of the angels. In the ensuing debate, Justice asserts that she will perish if Adam does not die; Mercy avers that she will be destroyed if he does not receive clemency. The Lord resolves the dilemma by His decision to make death good through the charity and innocence of His own Son. On pages which follow, miniatures narrating the lives of Christ and the Virgin continue in parallel sequence with episodes from the Old Testament which culminate in the need for redemption.

Painted during the second major campaign of illumination, these pages disclose Belbello's modifications of formal patterns established by his predecessor. Like Giovannino, he enjoys gold. He applies it to heavier designs, however, and in association with denser colors. Belbello also adopted from Giovannino the decorative use of architectural elements, often merged with plant forms. In the initial and frame enclosing the Fall of the Angels, undulant window motifs themselves assume the aspect of leaves.[19]

pro quibus effunдere preces decrcuimus.
quoscumque uel presens seculum adhuc in car
ne retinet uel futurum iam exutos corpo
re suscepit intercedentibus omnibus scis
tuis pietatis tue clementia omnium de
lictorum suorum ueniam consequantur.
P dominum nostrum ihesum christum filium tuum. ℣. ℟.
Exaudiat nos omnipotens et misericors
dominus. ℟. Amen.

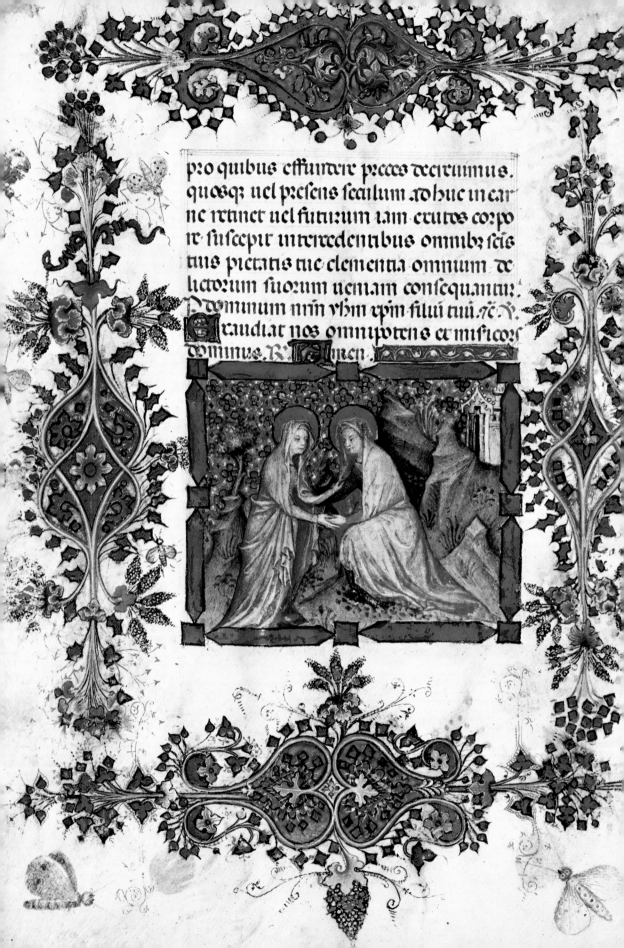

LF 17. Saints Ambrose and Augustine

The *Te Deum*, included in the Psalter (BR 148v), recurs on this folio as part of the Hours of the Virgin at Matins. Like its predecessor this miniature was painted during the fourteenth-century phase of illumination by Giovannino and his workshop. Again the hymn is illustrated by a representation of its purported authors. Here, however, they stand beneath boughs of an oak which constitutes the initial. Two human heads emerge from clusters of leaves on the trunk of the tree. Though rare, heads in trees occur earlier, most commonly in representations of Paradise.[20] The oak between Ambrose and Augustine may also be a tree of Paradise. Perhaps that is why its leaves remain verdant while the foliage in the borders is autumnal.

Numerous emblems of the Comte de Vertus appear in the acorn-strewn margins. Two of the Cardinal Virtues are paired on either side of a building surmounted by the Visconti crest: Prudence holds the calipers which identify her also on 11v; Justice, however, holds a sword rather than scales. Each of the Virtues displays the *biscia*, which also adorns the oaks at their sides. In the upper borders, scroll-bearing doves frame a Visconti sun.

The painting discloses several pentimenti. Augustine's red mantle has been widened over gold background, and part of the leaf which supports Prudence is visible beneath her left leg. Corrections have also partially obscured her three faces.

LF 18. *Annunciation to the Shepherds*

Like the earlier representation of this event in the borders of LF 11, the miniature on LF 18 was painted during the fifteenth-century campaign of illumination by Belbello da Pavia.

LF 18v. *Adoration of the Magi*

Amidst a dazzling array of color, the child, clothed simply in transparent white, blesses the kings. The Virgin gestures in amazement as the oldest magus tenderly raises the infant's foot to his lips. A royal purple cloak spills over one shoulder of the king's golden robe. He is characterized also, like his companions, by a scalloped nimbus distinct from those of the holy family. Beyond the space created by shed and fence, the retinue of the magi file between two steep hills. Like the crags behind them, from which they are not immediately distinguishable, these figures are modeled in red and blue against a green background lighted by gold. The midnight sky is illuminated not only by stars but also by golden haloes, stoles, and embroidered vesture of agitated angels. The pattern of glistening and saturated color which absorbs heaven and earth, inanimate and living forms, is of course not merely decorative. Like the menacing aspect of some of the figures, it is designed to dramatize sacred events.

Belbello's virtuoso display of drapery culminates in the prophets who adorn the borders. Architecture and sprays of golden foliage disclose the artist's intention to harmonize with his predecessor.

LF 19. *Creation of Heaven and Earth*

(HOURS OF THE VIRGIN. LAUDS)

The first episode of Creation introduces a series of initials illustrating the Book of Genesis and paired with full-page representations belonging to the narrative of the Virgin. (The text decorated, however, is not the Old Testament but rather a continuation of the Hours of the Virgin.) This arrangement adheres to the pattern established in the Psalter, where full-page paintings from the life of the Virgin are accompanied by initials introducing and illustrating the Psalms.

Like the portrait of David at the beginning of Psalm One (BR 3), the representation of God hovering over the deep is set against a radiant Visconti sun. Although both the book supported by a caryatid angel and the scroll beneath it refer to the making of heaven and earth, the D *(Deus)* and the borders are filled with other creations.

The comparatively rigid margins appear to be a late product of Giovannino's workshop. Corrections on this folio are even more numerous than those on LF 17. Architecture, apparently intended to reach into the upper margin, was supplanted on one side by a nesting bird (incubating its own small creation) and on the other by a book. Pentimenti are visible also behind the falcon at the upper left and the bird at the lower right who pecks at an insect on the bark of a tree. White outlines are unusually prominent around many of the forms.

tins gloria munerum. Saluum fac populu
tuu dne. 7 benedic hereditati tue. Et rege eo
7 extolle illos. usq; ineternum. Persingu
los dies benedicimus te. Et laudamus i
nomen tuum ineternum 7 inseculum secli.
Dignare dne die isto. sine peccato nos cu
stodire. Miserere nri dne miserere nostri.
Fiat mficordia tua dne supernos. quem
admodum sperauimus inte. Inte dne spe
raui. Non ofundar ineternum.

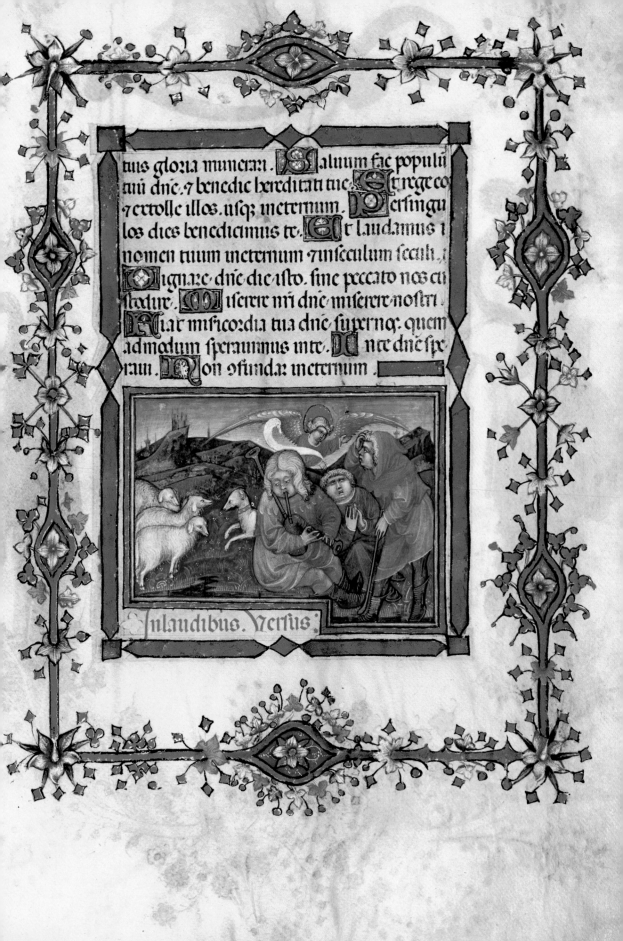

Inlaudibus. Versus

LF 25v.   *Flight into Egypt*

The holy family proceed along a stony path beside a stream. Mary is engrossed by her child, whose vulnerability is emphasized by his nakedness. Joseph, tanned and grizzle-bearded, carries a whip, a walking stick, and a canteen. He is addressed by an angel. The coarsely painted figures and imprecise diaper background characterize this folio as one of the more perfunctory contributions of the dei Grassi workshop to the Visconti Hours.

LF 26. *Separation of Firmament from the Waters*

(HOURS OF THE VIRGIN. PRIME)

In the firmament, the cross-nimbed Deity is surrounded by angels. A seraph above the initial holds a banderole. Its inscription, no longer legible, perhaps identified the act of creation. The D (*Deus*) is in the mode of earlier capitals (for example, BR 108v): small figures scramble within an architectural framework. At the top, one of them peers over a crenellated parapet at the pursuit below involving two men (one only partially clothed) and a dog. Another rushes toward a door at the upper left, accentuating the thrust of the stem which emerges from it, bearing nosegays of small blossoms set against gold. This folio was planned and painted by Giovannino's workshop. The novel green of the stem in the borders and three fleshy leaves in its apertures may disclose slight intervention by Belbello.

LF 29.   *Massacre of the Innocents*

To end the Office of Prime and introduce Terce, the Massacre of the Innocents is illustrated twice on this leaf, first by the workshop of Giovannino and then, on the verso, by Belbello. In the dei Grassi miniature, painted around the *explicit*, one mother tries to repel a soldier, while two others bewail their slain infants. Giangaleazzo's motto, *a buon droit*, fills four pairs of scrolls in the margins.

LF 29v.   *Massacre of the Innocents*

Belbello's *Massacre* again discloses his intention to conform with Giovannino's patterns. Several evocations of the earlier artist are strong enough to suggest that the later workshop completed a miniature partially painted by their predecessors. An original plan to include two *Massacres of the Innocents*, however, seems improbable. Herod is remarkably similar to the dei Grassi David on BR 120v. His face is unusually slender for Belbello, and the light brown curl falling onto his shoulder appears an afterthought to the short auburn hairstyle favored by the later artist. Herod's throne, inlaid with marquetry, closely resembles David's, and even the patterned cloth draped over it resembles a dei Grassi covering on BR 76v. The gold hanging behind Herod, however, is Belbello's. Two almost identical groups of a soldier with a defensive and a despairing mother are adaptations of the motif on the recto of this folio. Long tresses flowing onto the executioner's shoulders are again anachronistic. The blue dress of the woman at the upper right, modeled with small dabs of pigment and highlighted with large areas of white, is uncommon for Belbello but characteristic of the dei Grassi. Her green cloak, finely cross-hatched in yellow, is typical of Belbello. His also is the tiered, flower-strewn meadow on which the slaughter occurs. The night sky is filled with grieving angels, not so beautifully painted as their rejoicing counterparts on LF 18v.

   The motto *a buon droit* once more appears in the borders, set off here by peacock feathers. In the upper margin, rays of the sun encircle a dove. The same emblem recurs below, framed by a scroll of simulated script which also encloses four vipers. Rays visible around the scroll probably should have been gilded but were left incomplete.

LF 30.   *Separation of Land from Water*

(HOURS OF THE VIRGIN. TERCE)

For a discussion of this folio, see Part I of the Introduction.

equiem eternam concede. P dominum
nostrum yhesum xpm filium tuum qui te
cum uiuit z regnat inunitate sps sancti de
us p omnia secula seculorum. Amen . V.
omine exaudi orationem meam. R.
t clamor meus ad te ueniat. V.
enedicamus domino. R.
eo gratias. Psus.
t fidelium anime per misicordiam
dei requiescant inpace. Amen.

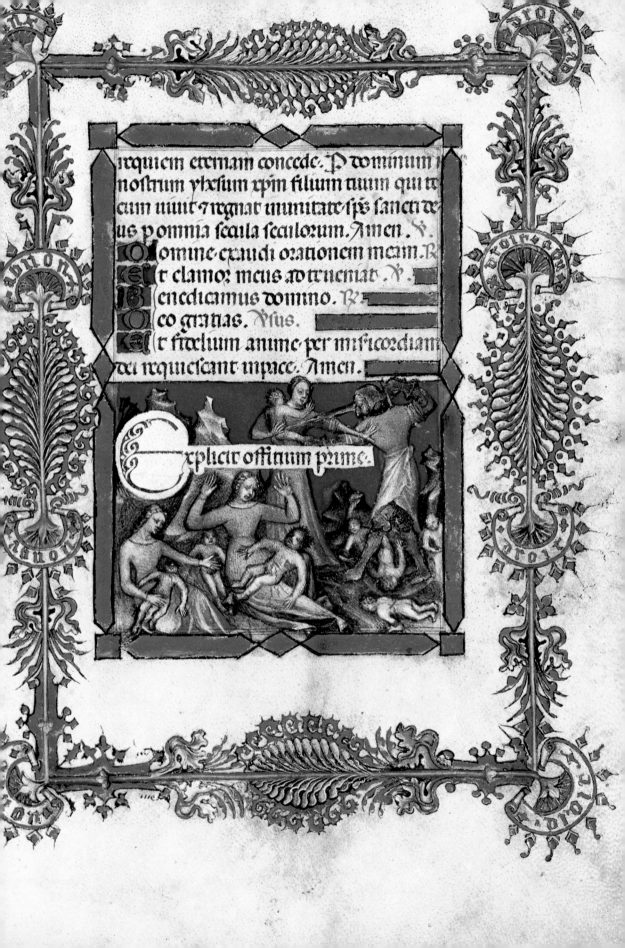

Explicit officium prime.

LF 33v.   *Annunciation of the Death of the Virgin*

Like the apocryphal narrative of the Virgin's youth, an uncanonical account of
the last events of her life became part of the *Golden Legend* (August 15, Assumption of the Virgin). Voragine relates that twelve years after the ascension
of her son, an angel appeared in the midst of a great light to tell Mary that after
three days, her soul, awaited by Christ, would be called forth from her body.
Representations of this scene are uncommon. In them, the angel, following the
text of the *Legend*, normally brings Mary a branch of the palm of Paradise.
Belbello's messenger, however, carries the stem of lilies (painted here in gilt
emulsion on burnished leaf) generally associated with the Annunciation of the
Incarnation. Nevertheless, both the advanced age of the Virgin and the position
of the miniature in the narrative sequence identify it as the annunciation of her
death.

An arrangement of color favored by Belbello—blue, green, and magenta,
combined with burnished gold—prevails in both miniature and borders. His
fascination with light employed for expressive purposes is apparent in glowing
wood and in the effect of divine rays upon the color of Mary's cloak. The trans-
parency of her wimple and translucency of her hands are familiar from preceding
folios (LF 11v, 18, 18v, 29v). The dramatic but spatially irrational structure which
shelters Mary is barely contained within the limits of the painting. On its ledge
is a glass carafe, a traditional attribute of the Virgin and symbolic of her purity.

LF 34.   *Creation of Trees and Plants*

Painted by Belbello, this folio once more may disclose both a design begun by the dei Grassi and a wish to conform with their style, particularly, in this instance, as it appears in preceding scenes of creation. The green architectural D (*Deus*) framed by a narrow pink band in the borders duplicates in transposed color the arrangement on LF 26. Caryatids supporting the architecture on LF 34, however, like the fine white cross-hatching of its components, are unmistakably Belbello's.

Plant life extends beyond the initial into the borders. The lacy, though rather stiff pattern of pale, gold-accented turrets, spires, and pinnacles adorned by sprays of gold-stamened flowers finds its origin in the borders of LF 30. Even the deep blue and rose blossoms in the right margin of LF 34 closely resemble their predecessors on LF 30. At the left, however, the colors of the flowers change. Turrets there extend farther into the upper border than their counterparts at the right, and they appear to be incompletely painted. Falcons perched in the upper margin are heavier in both design and color than Giovannino's (BR 48, 105).

LF 37. *Death of the Virgin*

At the Virgin's request, the apostles were miraculously plucked up by clouds from the places where they were preaching and brought to her so that she might see them once more before her death and return her spirit to God in their presence. In the miniature, the apostles are grouped at Mary's head and feet. Nearest the pillow are Peter and a long-bearded figure who probably represents Paul. The beardless youth at the right is John, the youngest apostle and adopted son of the Virgin. Hovering above the group in a rayed mandorla, God the Father embraces and returns the gaze of Mary's soul. The saturated colors of the painting, accented by small areas of lighter hues, brilliant red, gold, and white, are characteristic of Belbello.

The margins, though chromatically related to the miniature, are apparently unrelated to it in theme. At the right, St. George subdues the dragon who had been devouring the people of Silena. Following the saint's instructions, the princess has thrown her girdle about the serpent's neck in order to lead him back to her people like a dog on a leash. Belbello's painting conforms with the narrative in the *Golden Legend* (April 23, St. George), which says that the saint agreed to slay the dragon only after the baptism of the king and all his subjects. The upper border was designed and painted in part by the dei Grassi.

eus in adiu
torium meum intende. R̃ Domine. xo.xi
uandum me festina Gloria patri ⁊ filio.

LF 37v.   *Creation of Sun, Moon, and Stars*

And God said: Let there be lights made in the firmament of heaven, to divide the day and the night, and let them be for signs, and for seasons, and for days and years. (Genesis I:14)

The Deity hovers above the universe, which is depicted as a series of concentric circles. At the center is the earth. In the ocean around it are golden boats (their billowing white sails depicted with minuscule delicacy) and islands from which golden trees and turrets rise. Wispy clouds fill the firmament, irradiated by sun, moon, and stars. Zodiacal signs in the rim of the miniature (indications of the cycle of time) are complemented in the margins by personified seasons whose visual antecedents occur in earlier medieval as well as classical art. Seated in a kind of nest, Spring holds a spray of flowers. Summer displays a sheaf of golden grain, Autumn gathers grapes, and Winter warms his hands and feet at a fire. In the left border are the planets—Saturn, Jupiter, Mars, Venus, and Mercury—who also belong to an old tradition. They combine classical with medieval attributes: Saturn holds a scythe but is dressed as a warrior; Jupiter holds both the scepter of a ruler and the crozier of a bishop; Mercury, also represented as a Christian ecclesiastic, nevertheless retains his caduceus. Similar combinations characterize the widely copied thirteenth-century astronomico-astrological treatise of Michael Scot, which itself Christianizes Oriental elements traceable to the Babylonians.[21]

Belbello's cosmos is one of his finest contributions to the Visconti Hours. In it he does not fail to include family emblems, though they are far less prominent here than elsewhere. Doves appear in the initial D *(Deus)*, which terminates in two oak leaves, one of them framed by golden acorns.

LF 40v. *Obsequies of the Virgin*

Following the *Golden Legend*, the illuminator (a member of Giovannino's work-shop) portrays apostles carrying the Virgin's bier. John leads the procession, bearing the palm of Paradise. The cross-nimbed Deity, who holds Mary's soul, is surrounded by angels, described in the *Legend* as "filling the whole earth with the dulcity of their music." Two helmeted figures represent disbelievers whose hands wither as they attempt to overturn the bier.

LF 41. *Creation of Birds*

One of Belbello's most beautiful compositions depicts a Creator whose flowing hair, swirling drapery, and undulant scroll establish its rhythm. The turbulent waters beneath the Deity, like the ocean in the Creation of Sun, Moon, and Stars (LF 37v), are filled with ships and with islands bearing groves of trees and turreted buildings. Here, in addition, white birds hover above the sea. (Water may imply fish, who often accompany birds in creation cycles, but none are apparent in the miniature.) The principal objects of this episode of creation appear in the lower border. They include a variety of small birds as well as a peacock, stilt-birds, and predators, one of which has secured a duck beneath its talons.

Belbello's celebration of birds encompasses plumage in other forms. In the upper borders, bands of angels support Visconti helmets. The D *(Deus)* is dominated by an emblem new to this manuscript: a helmeted lion seated in flames and holding a branch from which two buckets are suspended. Whereas this device occurs earlier in the prayerbook illuminated between 1350 and 1378 for Giangaleazzo's mother, Blanche of Savoy (Munich, Staatsbibliothek, lat. 23215), the lions' helmets there lack the exuberant wings given them by Belbello.

The lions here surmount acanthus "capitals" at the terminals of a twisted ribbon which enhances the sinuous movement of the page. This rhythm is further emphasized by pink, white, and green clouds enclosing the *biscia* and by arabesques of ivy and flowers, some of whose petals frame additional vipers.

The principal colors of the page—pink, blue, green, and purple, all set off by gold—are recapitulated in the secondary initials and in the delicate strip of blossoms separating the second and third lines of text.

Ad uesperas offitium. Iesus

LF 46v. *Creation of Eve*

Adam lies fast asleep as Eve arises toward the Creator. The Deity, surrounded by angels painted in gold emulsion on foil, holds a silver scroll as in the preceding miniature. His face is again framed by flowing white hair, and He wears a similar blue mantle lighted by fine strokes of white. Here, however, Belbello introduces a brilliant red tunic which, like the wings of the griffin in the border, is brought into bold proximity with the fuchsia terrain of the C *(Converte)*. Animals created before man inhabit the initial and the borders. These include domestic as well as exotic species in addition to the fabulous griffin.

Ivy arabesques and clusters of fruit-bearing trees recall earlier folios of Belbello (LF 11, 41). Precipitous hills and the golden grape "tree" at the right, however, were probably inspired by the dei Grassi (BR 115, 124v, LF 30).

LF 47. *The Lord in Majesty*

The Lord rests, holding in one hand a small world and in the other a book, suggesting that He created all things with a word. Haloed figures, probably representing prophets and apostles, stand on pedestals within tabernacles at either side of the Deity. In the borders, radiant gold clouds support bands of angels, each group painted in a different color. They may refer to six of the nine celestial choirs often represented in attendance upon the Lord. The rose group at the upper right is led by the Archangel Michael, holding the sword of justice as well as the scales with which he weighs human souls. The cluster of green angels at the left may allude to the Principalities, who are sometimes shown holding tapers. From each of the clouds a silver scroll emerges bearing the motto *a bon droyt* (partly lost in several instances).

Most of the folio, including God the Father, the angels, and even the decoration of the script, belongs clearly to Belbello. The flourish at the upper left of the D *(Deus)*, however, different from the foliage framing the initial, closely resembles leaves attributable to the dei Grassi (LF 51).

ONUERTENOS

deus salutaris noster. V. Et auerte

iram tuam anobis. Versus.

LF 50v. *Coronation of the Virgin*

The narrative of the Virgin in the Visconti Hours concludes with her coronation in heaven. Within a burnished mandorla, Christ and his mother share a green throne partially covered in scarlet. Blue pillows beneath their feet extend the color of their abundantly draped clothing. The ceremony is witnessed by magenta angels whose intense faces are modeled in white. One of them blows a Visconti trumpet.

Four saints appear within almond-shaped openings in the arabesque of the borders. Catherine of Alexandria and John the Baptist stand at the sides, the latter traditionally gesturing toward the Savior. Both John and Catherine were frequently represented in the fourteenth and fifteenth centuries, but in the Visconti Hours they may have special significance as patrons of Giangaleazzo and his wife Caterina. The bishop in the lower margin might be Ambrose, patron of Milan. The identity of the saint above, cramped by his frame, is far less certain. Apostles, however, are commonly depicted with veiled hands (see, for example, the figure at the right in LF 37). If this figure too is an apostle, he may represent Barnabas, an even earlier patron of the city.

Though executed with less care than the miniature, the borders also are painted in the style of Belbello. The design of the arabesque framed by gold lozenges, however, suggests the dei Grassi workshop. It was undoubtedly planned to harmonize with the borders on the facing folio.

LF 51. *Original Sin*

The miniature introduces the first of three Psalms (XLIV, XLV, and LXXXVI) rubricated on folio 50 for recitation on Tuesday and Friday as part of the Hours of the Virgin. It portrays the event which created the need for redemption, whose principal protagonists—the new Adam and the new Eve—appear in glory on the facing folio in the presence of saints. Earthly Paradise, on the other hand, is embellished by emperors and kings.

The dei Grassi nudes on LF 51 are more delicate than their counterparts by Belbello on LF 46v. Their nudity concealed by drapery-like foliage and their bodies modeled with small strokes of green, Adam and Eve here seem an organic part of the Garden of Eden. The E *(Eructavit)* and its extensions in the border move with freedom characteristic of earlier pages by Giovannino and his shop. Stylized gold leaves, some of them oak-like, also resemble their predecessors (BR 22v, 115, 145).

RUOTHUILOOR
meum uerbum bonum dico ego opera
mea regi lingua mea calamus scri

LF 54.   *The Lord Reproaches Adam and Eve*

This is the last page in the Visconti Hours containing a miniature painted by the dei Grassi. It is also the first to display the monogram of Giangaleazzo's son, Filippo Maria, for whom the manuscript was completed. Like the monogram, some of the exceptionally numerous armorials on this folio (such as the shield at the upper right) appear to be later additions. The motto *a buon droyt* is superimposed on the first line of text in syncopated and erratic form. The extensive heraldry is probably best understood as a link to Giangaleazzo's manuscript added in the fifteenth century by Filippo Maria's illuminator.

In the final contribution of the dei Grassi, Adam and Eve hide behind a slope from which a gnarled tree grows almost as an extension of their bodies. Behind them, a stag emerges from a verdant grove surmounted by fluttering birds. In the foreground, part of the Creator's mantle falls onto a grassless plateau outside the precincts of Paradise. The delicate architectural C *(Cantate)* is still another reminder of Giovannino's inventiveness.

The miniature introduces Psalms XCV through XCVII, rubricated on LF 53v for recitation on Wednesday and Saturday. They conclude the basic text for the Hours of the Virgin, which is supplemented by variants (Propers), beginning on LF 57v, for different seasons of the liturgical year.

LF 57v and 58.   *Transference of Blame*

(PROPER FOR ADVENT. MATINS)

These miniatures belong to a continuous pictorial tradition, traceable to the Early Christian period, in which Adam blames Eve and Eve blames the serpent for their transgression. The presence of mankind's progenitors perhaps suggested to the illuminator a condensed genealogy of the Visconti as decoration of the borders on 57v. The profile at the top may represent Anchises, from whom the Visconti claimed descent. At the sides are pairs of veiled profiles (perhaps women), wreathed men, and youths. The bust in the center of the lower margin probably represents Filippo Maria, portrayed like his father (BR 115) within a ring of pink and blue clouds set against golden rays. This painting depicts a much younger man than the portrait of Filippo Maria by Pisanello on the medal of around 1441.

It is not surprising that the second patron should have wished to be portrayed on the opening miniature of the first gathering of leaves in the Visconti Hours illuminated entirely for him. The display of armorials which continues on the facing folio comprises vipers in the initial and numerous scroll-bearing doves in the margins, including two beneath tabernacles at the sides. The child triumphant over a lion in the lower margin is probably meant to suggest the power of the Duke.

OMINE LABIA

mea aperies. R̃ . Et os meum

annunciabit laudem tuam. Versus.

torum meum intende R̅ omic

ad adiuuandum me festina

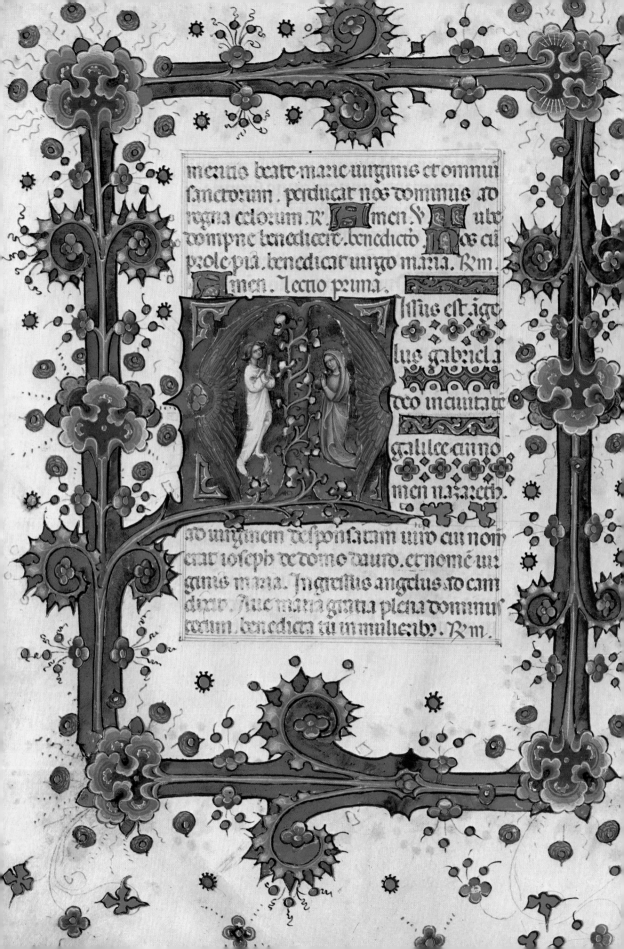

mento beate marie virginis et omnui
sanctorum. perducat nos dominus ad
regna celorum. R. Amen. V. Iube
domine benedicere. benedicto Nos cii
prole pia. benedicat virgo maria. R m.
Amen. lectio prima.

Missus est ange
lus gabriel a
deo in civitate
galilee cuino
men nazareth.

ad virginem desponsatam viro cui nomi
erat ioseph de domo david. et nome vir
ginis maria. Ingressus angelus ad eam
dixit. Aue maria gratia plena dominus
tecum. benedicta tu in mulieribus. R m.

LF 59v.　The Annunciation

The M (*Missus*) introduces and illustrates the first lesson of the Proper for Matins in Advent (Luke 1: 26–28). Closely related in color and design to LF 57v and 58, this folio owes its more delicate effect to the refinement of its miniature and the integration of its components, including decorated bands between lines of text. A stem of the border grows into the initial where it twines around the tree that constitutes the central stroke of the letter. Although Gabriel's wings are depicted in gold emulsion against a burnished background, two additional pairs of gold-shot blue wings appear as part of the initial. Mary wears a traditional blue mantle over a green robe whose color is uncanonical. A blue mantle over green, however, is common in the Madonnas of Michelino da Besozzo, another fifteenth-century illuminator employed by the Visconti, whose work Belbello must have known.

LF 61v.　Expulsion from Paradise

(PROPER FOR ADVENT. LAUDS)

Holding a baton but lacking His halo, the Deity drives Adam and Eve, now clothed, out of Eden. The landscape, green and brown with gold highlights in the foreground, dissolves into pure gold in the distance. A solitary green tree emphasizes the direction forced upon the sinners. Angels painted in gold emulsion hover in the sky, while a fiery red seraph prepares to guard the golden gates of Paradise, which are closing. (An object perhaps intended to be a sword is drawn above the seraph but was never painted.) Winged putti on parapets of the D (*Deus*) flee from vipers in the borders.

LF 64.　Adam and Eve Delve

(PROPER FOR ADVENT. PRIME)

Conventional representations of the labor of Adam and Eve show Adam delving and Eve spinning or suckling a child. The Visconti miniature, however, which depicts both parents holding mattocks, follows a Lombard tradition at least as old as the early twelfth-century sculpture by Wiligelmo on the facade of Modena Cathedral. The folio is painted with meticulous care. It is distinguished not only by refined use of punched gold leaf and gold emulsion, but also by extensive employment of silvery pigment in the armor of St. George, in the glazed tunic of St. Christopher, and, spectacularly combined with gold, in the mantle and pillow of the king (probably David) and the hills around him.

eos in adiu
torium meum intende. R̄. Domine
ad adiuuandum me festina. Gloria

utorium meum intende. R̃ Domine
ad adiuuandum me festina, Gloria
patri 7 filio 7 spiritui sancto. Sicut

LF 66. *Sacrifice of Cain and Abel*

(PROPER FOR ADVENT. TERCE)

Cain and Abel make their offering at an altar whose front and end panels are decorated with saints and the Virgin and Child. The Lord points disapprovingly toward Cain's sacrifice, but the grain which should appear on the cloth is lacking. Abel, incorrectly portrayed as the older brother, offers the customary firstlings of his flock. He wears an aquamarine mantle over a pale blue tunic, banded like the Deity's with simulated script. The Lord's halo, painted in gold emulsion, is modeled in depth, its volume emphasized by curves in the cross which adorns it. The initial, consisting of mauve and green architectural forms combined with foliage, is set against a tessellated background similar to those on LF 58 and 64. Like the haloes of Evangelist symbols in the borders and rays of the sun behind the miniature, each small gold square is punched. Colored squares alternating with the gold change from green to blue in harmony with the principal colors of the initial. The delicate hues of the miniature pervade also the first line of text, whereas decorative bands between subsequent lines are painted in the bolder colors predominant in the margins.

Multi-winged Evangelist symbols exemplify the illuminator's predilection for superimposed planes of various colors. The angel of Matthew and eagle of John stand on green pedestals in front of punched gold bands. Symbols in the lower border, resting on the Gospels of Mark and Luke, flank the dove of the Holy Spirit, who inevitably suggests a family emblem. The untarnished scroll held by Mark's lion may have been painted with a substitute for silver, perhaps tin.[22]

Eus in adiutorium meum intende. R. Domine ad adiuuandum me festina. Gloria patri et filio et spiritui sancto. Sicut

LF 68. *Cain Murders Abel*

(PROPER FOR ADVENT. SEXT)

Cain prepares to strike Abel in a landscape as rigid as the figures it contains. The older brother stands in an awkward contrapposto, like a mannequin displaying drapery. The stippled painting of his cap and the lining of Abel's mantle recall miniatures by the dei Grassi, but Abel's light brown robe, delicately modeled and embroidered in yellow, is characteristic of Belbello. Both the foliate D *(Deus)* and sprays in the borders are painted in an untarnished silvery pigment. A scroll of blue, green, and mauve leaves on a burnished gold background unifies the miniature and first line of text. Visconti shields appear within quatrefoils in the initial and again in the borders, where they are framed by layers of blue and mauve petals surrounded by a kind of calyx painted in gold-speckled brown. As in preceding folios by this illuminator, the petals, which are modeled in white, curl forward to suggest volume.

LF 70.   *Lamech Slays Cain*

(PROPER FOR ADVENT. NONE)

After murdering his brother, Cain lived for many years as a fugitive. He begot a line of sons and was eventually murdered by his own great-great-great grandson, Lamech. In Genesis 4:23 Lamech himself tersely describes the event: "I have slain a man to the wounding of myself, and a stripling to my own bruising." The Visconti illuminator depicts the fuller account of this episode given in the twelfth-century *Historia Scholastica* of Peter Comestor, a history of the world from Creation through the Acts of the Apostles, in which the Old Testament, Gospels, and Acts are supplemented by commentaries of the author.[23] According to the *Historia Scholastica*, Lamech, being blind, takes a boy with him to guide his hand in hunting. The boy mistakes Cain, concealed among trees, for a beast and guides Lamech's arrow to kill him. Realizing that he has killed his own ancestor, Lamech later slays his guide.

The murder of Cain occurs here in a hilly, turreted landscape highlighted in blue and red as well as gold. A green and gold tree against a graded blue sky reinforces the fatal direction of the arrow. Lamech, though he does not appear blind, is anatomically more successful than his predecessor on LF 68. He wears an exotic cap intended to suggest his Eastern origins and remoteness in time. A nearby church, however, is Western and medieval. Its roof, like those in the outline of the initial, is silver. Simulated Arabic script embellishes the frame in the borders.

EUS INAVIU

torum meum intende. ℟. Domine
ad adiuuandum me festina. Gloria

LF 72. *Noah Guides Animals into the Ark*

The patriarch wears a bright red cap and blue tunic, both embroidered with pseudo-script. Full white sleeves are swathed around his arms. The colors of his costume reappear in a pair of ostriches who, together with camels, lions, and cheetahs, accompany domestic species including stags, boars, sheep, and rabbits. On a ledge of the three-storey ark, a pair of monkeys ignore the flood which has already engulfed all but the silvery domes and turrets of a city in the foreground and threatens a second town, painted entirely in red with silver roofs, at the upper right. Several human bodies float in waves at the top of the miniature.

Numerous armorials on this folio include Filippo Maria's monogram and many vipers. The central shield, which quarters the biscia with the eagle of the Holy Roman Empire, was the ducal insignia of Milan. Oak leaves in the lower border recur beneath warrior angels at the sides. Visconti suns illumine blue clouds in the margins and also frame shields in quatrefoils of the initial.

LF 74. *Abraham Sacrificing Isaac*

(PROPER FOR ADVENT. COMPLINE)

In conformity with iconographic convention, the Lord's messenger saves Isaac from his father's knife, and a substitute holocaust appears in the form of a ram. The grill in the Visconti miniature, however, resembling the instrument of death common in representations of the martyrdom of St. Lawrence, replaces the altar traditional to the Sacrifice. Firewood, a normal component of the scene, here feeds flames through an arched opening below the rack. Although the perspective of the grill is unpersuasive, its glowing color is an effective foil for Isaac's nude body and Abraham's rose shawl. The patriarch is a powerful figure. He holds his son's head with one large hand, while the other is restrained by the much smaller hand of the angel. An apron knotted at his ample waist is a painfully practical accessory.

Metallic surfaces, which pervade the folio, include a pointillist silver and blue sky as well as numerous silver shields and scrolls. Burnished gold glitters throughout the miniature and the borders.

ratam sibi in nobis inueniat mansionem.
Qui tecum uiuit et regnat deus. 7c. V.
Domine exaudi orationem meam. R.
Et clamor meus ad te ueniat. V. **B**e
nedicamus domino. V. **D**eo gratias.
Fidelium aie pmisicordiam dei requie
scant in pace. R. **A**men. ad completoriu.

deus saluc̃ne nr̃ **E**t auerce iram tuã

anobis.

eus inadiu to
rum meum intente. ❧ omine
ad adminandum me festina. Glona

LF 74v. *Isaac Blesses Jacob*

The Proper for Compline in Advent is illustrated by a second miniature, showing Jacob, his hands disguised by a lambskin, usurping from his blind, dying father the blessing intended for his older brother, Esau (Genesis 27:21–29). The boy's mother, Rebecca, encourages him. Aspects of domesticity in the miniature include a cat beside the bed, a silver pitcher and basin on its ledge, a second pitcher in a niche, and violets growing on balconies beneath blue and silver roofs in the initial. The illuminator's skill in painting a variety of cloths is apparent in the densely modeled counterpane and the crisp white folds of Rebecca's veil. Filmy gold lighting of the aged man's blue robe contrasts with the soft modeling in green and rose of Jacob's scalloped yellow tunic.

LF 78v. *Joseph, His Brothers, and the Ishmaelites*

Following the Office of the Virgin and unassociated with text, three miniatures from the story of Joseph complete a gathering and conclude the Visconti Genesis cycle. In the opening sequence, Joseph hovers in a wicker basket above the cistern into which he is cast by his brothers and from which they later withdraw him to sell him to Ishmaelite merchants (Genesis 37:23–28). The substantial well in the miniature, conveniently fitted with a winch, is a pictorial transformation of the dry pit mentioned in the biblical text. Absence of water is suggested, however, by a dry riverbed. Ishmaelites appear on horseback at the right. The city below may represent Egypt, where the merchants will sell Joseph to Potiphar.

LF 79. *Joseph and Potiphar's Wife*

Resisting the advances of his master's wife, Joseph hastens toward the threshold of a door which he seems to have pushed open with his left elbow. He is unable, however, to free his mantle from the woman's grasp. The seductress has made the temptation as inviting as possible. Plump pillows and a flowered cover adorn the bed beneath the star-strewn ceiling of her chamber. The lady herself wears a crown and a richly embroidered gown of alluring décolletage. A verdant landscape, visible at the sides of the house and through a loggia at the rear, enhances the sensuousness of the scene.

LF 79v. *Joseph Blesses His Family*

The miniature suggests a familiar episode in the Joseph cycle: his brothers making obeisance to him in Egypt. The figure wearing a hat, who stands apart and looks away from the family, perhaps represents Joseph's Egyptian steward. Since the brothers are recently arrived from Canaan, one of them carries a traveling bag across his chest. Novel and puzzling, however, is the presence of an old man and woman in Belbello's miniature. Joseph's mother died before his abduction by his brothers. His father, when he joins Joseph in Egypt, blesses others but does not himself receive a blessing. A dream recounted early in his life by Joseph, however, may clarify the meaning of the painting.

> I saw in a dream, as it were the sun, and the moon, and eleven stars worshipping me.
> And when he had told this to his father and brethren, his father rebuked him and said: What meaneth this dream that thou hast dreamed? shall I and thy mother, and thy brethren worship thee upon the earth? (Genesis 37:9–10)

The Visconti miniature, therefore, though narratively incorrect, is spiritually and symbolically appropriate. The Annunciation in the spandrels of Joseph's palace makes explicit the Christian interpretation of him as a type of Christ.

LF 80. *Baptism of Christ*

(OFFICE OF THE DEAD. VESPERS)

The Old Testament cycle in the Visconti Hours continues with a pictorial narrative of Exodus through the beginning of I Kings 3. Preceding the first miniature of Moses, however, is a symbolic episode from the New Testament appropriate to the Office it introduces. The association between baptism and death in Christian thought goes back to its origins. St. Paul described baptism as burial with Christ (Rom. 6:3–4), and the Savior himself twice refers to his own impending death as a baptism (Mark 10:38, Luke 12:50). Death was regarded as a second baptism, a purging of evil which completed the spiritual rebirth of baptism by water.

In Belbello's miniature, the Jordan flows down from the top of a landscape bathed in morning sun. The river is painted in silver, gold, and green. Rushes grow along its banks; birds and even a boat with a two-man crew skim along its surface. Christ is more delicately modeled than the nude Adam on LF 57v. Elegant folds of his loincloth accentuate the elongation of his body. The Baptist's disheveled hair and gauntness contrast with the soft fullness of a pair of angels whose colors are exceptionally balanced and harmonious. One of the golden rays emanating from the Lord strikes the baptismal vessel, but the dove of the Holy Spirit, normally present in this scene (see BR 145), is absent. Both the miniature and borders of this folio complement the design of the facing page.

Incipit offitium mortuorum. Ad ue
speras. antiphona.

Antiphona. Aduesperas.
Placebo domino. psalmus dauid.

eraudiet dns. uocem orationis mee. Quia
inclinauit aurem suam michi. 7 indiebus

LF 80v.   Moses Placed in Nile and
Returned by Pharaoh's Daughter

Two episodes from the life of Moses are combined in this initial. In the first, his
mother places him in the river to save him from Pharaoh's fatal decree against
sons of Hebrew women. Then, Pharaoh's daughter, having found the child, brings
him unknowingly to his mother to be nursed (Exodus 2:3–9).

A crown and scepter distinguish the princess from her ladies in waiting.
The faces of all the women, however, are Belbellesque paradigms, characterized
by full cheeks and by prominent white in the eyes, along the ridge of the nose,
above the mouth, and in the chin. In keeping with the predominantly mauve and
blue tones of the page, the faces here are modeled with rose rather than the more
orange red of the two preceding miniatures. Blue and rose also glaze silver in the
doves, their scrolls, and Visconti shields.

LF 84v.   Moses Slays an Egyptian

(OFFICE OF THE DEAD. FIRST NOCTURN)

Moses prepares to kill the already wounded assailant of a Hebrew who looks re-
proachfully at his tormentor (Exodus 2:11–12). Shells and pebbles on the Egyptian's back may correspond to the text, which says that Moses, after slaying his
victim, hid him in the sand.

Heavier design distinguishes this and the facing page (its pendant in form
and color) from immediately preceding folios. The riverbank, gleaming towers
silhouetted against the sky, and the brown crag which parallels Moses' club are
motifs familiar from earlier miniatures. Rocks nearer the foreground, however,
are modeled more naturalistically than their predecessors.

Below the miniature, the initial R (Regem) is flanked by a small Visconti
shield and dove.

LF 85.   Moses and the Burning Bush

The Lord addresses Moses from a flaming bush on Mt. Horeb, where the young
Israelite has brought his father-in-law's sheep to graze: "Come not nigh hither,
put off the shoes from thy feet: for the place whereon thou standest is holy
ground" (Exodus 3:5). Beneath the mountain, a mauve bridge crosses a winding
silver river. A fortress soars against the sky at the upper left. Nearby, a golden
stream turns a mill between brown and purple hills.

scīs tuis ad perpetue beatitudinis consortiū
peruenire conceedas.

In agenda mortuorum. Ad matutinum
Inuitatorium. Regem cui omnia ui
uunt. Uenite adoremus . psalmus . dauid.

enite exul
temus domino. iubilemus deo salutari nio. pre
occupemus faciem eius in confessione ampla

LF 85v.   *Rod of Moses Changed to a Serpent*

The miniature illustrates a subsequent moment in the encounter between Moses and the Lord that begins on the previous folio. To encourage the young shepherd in his mission as leader of the Israelites, the Deity transforms his staff into a serpent (Exodus 4:3). Moses flees the winged creature (no ordinary snake of the garden variety common to this scene), which writhes from the tip of its tongue to the end of its long, looped tail. The monster dominates but does not obscure the beauty of the landscape around him. Familiar gold fences wind through hills graded from green through gray to brown. Sheep of various sizes continue to graze beneath the burning bush. A single bright red building stands out from the gold and burgundy city outlined against a silvery blue sky similar to the firmament in the *Sacrifice of Isaac* (LF 74).

The initial V *(Venite)* is a composite of foliate architecture comprising parapets, balconies, staircases, and a tabernacle, beneath which a nimbed figure, presumably a prophet, holds a red book. Viper shields at either side of the letter recur in two corners of the margins where they are framed by haloed, fiery red angels. Blue escutcheons in opposite corners display, at the lower left, a scroll-bearing dove within a rayed sun and, at the upper right, an emblem new to this manuscript but found in others belonging to Filippo Maria Visconti: a knotted cloth *(nodo)* enclosing the scroll-bearing dove within rays and surmounted by a crown through which branches of palm and laurel emerge.[24]

LF 89.   *Meeting of Moses and Aaron*

A twin-towered P *(Parce)* introduces the first lesson of the Office of the Dead (Job 7: 16–21). The scene framed by the initial, however, is unrelated to this text. Instead, it continues the Exodus sequence, showing the embrace of Moses with Aaron, sent by the Lord to assist him (Exodus 4:27). The faces of the figures, modeled with much white, stand out against a novel landscape, painted entirely in black and gold.

In the borders, the illuminator again combines deep pink and blue with a variety of metallic surfaces (see also LF 80v). Gold sprays enclose roseate blossoms similar to those on LF 58 and 59v, and silver shields display vipers outlined by arabesques of silvery emulsion.

LF 90v.   *Miracle of the Rods*

Belbello here portrays two moments from the episode in which Moses and Aaron first demonstrate their power before Pharaoh (Exodus 7:7–12). At the left, the young shepherd, holding his staff and accompanied by an apprehensive Aaron, demands admission to Pharaoh's presence. The audacity of Moses' act is emphasized by the height to which he must extend his arm in order to reach the doorknocker; gold embroidery at his shoulder underscores the importance of his gesture. Within, the Israelite's rod, again transformed to a serpent, vanquishes a similar iridescent reptile created by one of the Egyptian sorcerers. Magicians surrounding their golden-robed king are astounded. So, too, is Aaron. The illuminator has modified details of the text, which says that Moses and Aaron were eighty and eighty-three years old at the time of the event and gives Aaron a more prominent role in it.

Pharaoh's palace is a decorative structure which reiterates the colors of the actors' clothing. Particles of gold glisten in the ceiling and the door, which is framed by black and white voussoirs. Silver adorns the roofs. Both metals sparkle in the windows of the curved apse at one end of the audience chamber.

LF 91.   *Plague of Hail*

(OFFICE OF THE DEAD. SECOND NOCTURN)

Formally similar to representations of Christ in the Garden of Gethsemane, the miniature shows Moses asking the Lord to end the plague of hail (Exodus 9:33). The dark upper half of the landscape is lighted in gold against a menacing silvery sky. Below, Egyptians and their animals cower in a heap beneath the storm. One of the victims, beautifully clothed in an amethyst mantle over a blue and white tunic, lies fallen on one of his cattle. In the frame of the borders, the gold crowns of Filippo Maria alternate with the *biscia*.

℣. A porta inferi. ℟. Erue dñe
animas eorum. ℣. Pater nr. ℣. Et
ne nos inducas intemptationem. ℟.
Sed libera nos amalo. Amen. lc. j.

Parce michi do
mine michil em
sunt dies mei.
Quid est homo
quia magnifica
eum. aut qd ap
ponis erga eum
cor tuum. Uisita
eum diluculo. ꝫ
subito probas illu. Usq; quo
non parcis michi. nec dimittis
me ut glutiam saliuam meam.
Peccaui. Quid faciam tibi o cu
stos hominum. quare posuisti
me contrarium tibi. ꝫ factus sũ
metipi grauis. Cur non tollis
peccatum meum. ꝫquare non

quia peccaui nimis in uita mea. Requi
em eternam dona eis domine: et lux perpetua
luceat eis. Quia peccaui nimis. in uita mea.

Explicit offin primi nocturni.

In secdo nocturno. a ✠ In loco pascue. ps.

OMIИVSREGIT

me · 7 nichil michi de erit. in loco pascue. ibi
me collocauit. S up aquam reffectiois

LF 95.   *Plague of the Firstborn*

A tidy snowfall, not mentioned in the text, blankets Belbello's setting of the final plague (Exodus 12:21–30). Unusual also is the presence of a devil who assists the angel in performing the task. Here the demon is directed to an Egyptian household in which a young man lies on his deathbed, surrounded by grieving relatives. The letter *tau* on the door of the house at the left identifies it as Israelite, therefore to be spared by the angel of death. Residents within have begun their departure.

tibi. opperi manuum tuarum porriges dex
teram. Tu quidem gressus meos dinume
rasti. sz parce peccatis. R̃. Ne recorde
ris peccata mea domine. Dum ueneris i
iudicare seculum per ignem. Ṽ. Diri
ge domine deus meus in conspectu tuo
uiam meam. Dum ueneris. Requiem
eternam. dona eis domine. Alux perpetua
luceat eis. Dum ueneris iudicare: Tc.

Expliat offinum secudi nocturni.

LF 95v. *Israelites Leave Egypt*

In the distance, two golden figures stand in a doorway and a third crosses a draw-bridge which leads the Israelites away from the silver towers of Egypt. As the Hebrews descend, they pass between strips of gold terrain and groves of trees which, like the figures, curve into the lower half of the initial. A motif common to Exodus scenes is the woman who holds one child in a sling at her waist and leads a second by the hand. Beside her, a bearded man carrying a bag across his chest bends forward under the weight of a second pack on his shoulder. A young boy following him carries a pitcher.

The luxuriantly foliate initial of *Expectans* envelops a haloed king, probably David. Simple ivy scrolls in the borders complement the dense miniature and initial. Unusually elaborate penwork embellishes the catchword *miserie*.

LF 99.   *Israelites Pass through the Red Sea*

Pharaoh's army descends upon terrified Israelites. One of the Hebrews holds a cloth-covered basket, perhaps containing unleavened bread, construed in Christian theology as the antecedent of the sacramental host. In the upper half of the miniature, the Egyptians advance against a strong wind which fills the sail of a small boat nearby (a second boat in the lower zone drifts with its sail furled). Pharaoh's soldiers wear a variety of headdress, including helmets. He himself wears a peaked turban whose form is restated by blossoms throughout the borders. Clouds in the initial S *(Spiritus)* probably refer to the pillar of cloud which guided the Iraelites and obscured them from their pursuers. Part of the Third Nocturn, the initial introduces the seventh lesson in the Office of the Dead (Job 17).

LF 101v.   *Pharaoh's Army Drowned*

Moses, now white-haired and bearded, extends his rod, causing the sea to swallow Pharaoh's army; Israelites, painted with gem-like brilliance, proceed along the shore, immured from the cataclysm by an emphatic strip of green terrain. In the distance, Egypt stands deserted. Belbello's portrayal of the Egyptians' demise discloses his flair for the comic as well as the disastrous. Some of the soldiers attempt to stay afloat with a breaststroke; others, nearer the foreground, are already submerged to their mouths. The chariot rolls over one dandy wearing a feathered boater. A second, entangled in his scarf, floats on his back. Still another goes down head first. One of the charioteers waves his hands in despair, while his companion brandishes a whip in one hand and clutches the reins of his horse with the other.

Scorpions, emblazoned on the chariot and pennants, often appear in Christian art as heraldic identification of the enemies of God's people. On this folio, they also contrast with the ubiquitous Visconti viper.

LF 102.   *Moses Receives the Ten Commandments*

(OFFICE OF THE DEAD. LAUDS)

Kneeling on the slopes of an alpine Mt. Sinai, Moses dominates the painting by virtue of his brilliant red cloak and conspicuous bald head. (A tree sprouting improbably at a second level from the grove behind him further enhances his prominence.) The Lawgiver appears in half-length within a radiant mandorla.

Oratories, trees, and long-bearded worthies in the terraced M *(Miserere)* suggest the influence of the dei Grassi initial on LF 19. Belbello's figures, however, wearing garments embroidered with simulated Eastern script, represent Old Testament patriarchs rather than hermits. The king in the central stroke of the initial, similar to his counterpart on LF 95v, is clearly identified here by his psaltery as David. Formal integration of the monochromatic patriarchs with the protagonists of the miniature is subtle and distinctive. The figure in profile at the right, for example, simultaneously emphasizes the Deity and reflects the attitude of Moses.

meus attenuabitur. dies mei breuabunt
7 solum michi super est sepulchrum. Nam
peccaui. 7 inamaritudinibg moratur oculus
meus. Libera me domine et pone me iusta
te. 7 cui uis manus pugnet contra me. 1
Dies mei transierunt cogitationes mee
dissipate sunt torquentes cor meum. Noc

SEREREMEI

deus. scdm magnam misicordiá tuam.

Et scdm multitudinem miseracionu

LF 109v. *Adoration of the Golden Calf*

Having already broken one of the tablets of the law, Moses, his brows knit in anger, prepares to hurl the second to the foot of the mountain, where Israelites worship their impious idol (Exodus 32:19). The landscape, unusually extensive even for Belbello, is suffused by gold which, in one of its many worldly manifestations, has beguiled the Hebrews (and perhaps also the author of the miniature). Genre elements include a mill, a water-carrier, and a woman riding sidesaddle on a donkey. In the borders, arabesques of ivy on wide bands of gold frame Visconti scrolls which curl back at intervals to expose familiar four-petaled flowers.

LF 110. *Punishment of Korah and His Company*

(SEVEN PENITENTIAL PSALMS)

The miniature probably illustrates the punishment by fire and earthquake of Korah and his faction, who rebelled against the authority of Moses and Aaron (Numbers 16). The setting of the event within the sanctuary is unusual; it normally occurs outdoors, but the tabernacle in which the rebels offered incense is sometimes included in the background. The only figure unpunished in the miniature presumably represents Aaron in his priestly raiment. He points to the altar, which is again anachronistically adorned with an image of the Madonna and Child (see also LF 66).

The portrayal of transgression punished is an appropriate introduction to the Seven Penitential Psalms. Reiteration of the Visconti motto, *a bon droyt*, in the scroll which constitutes the D *(Domine)*, as well as in banderoles borne by doves, seems in this context an incantation against wrongdoing.

Incipit septem psalmi penitentales ant.
Ne reminiscaris domine. psalmus.

DomineNeIn
furore tuo arguas me. neqʒ ira tua cor
ripias me Miserere mei domine quo

LF 117v. *God Gives the Israelites Water*

> *And when Moses had lifted up his hand, and struck the rock twice with the rod, there came forth water in great abundance, so that the people and their cattle drank. . . . (Numbers 20:11)*

Water pouring from the rock and from the cupped hand of the drinking boy creates sparkling gold droplets as it splashes into the pool. In the foreground, a cow, encouraged by Moses, also quenches its thirst. Like the bovine members of his flock, the patriarch is distinguished here (as he frequently is elsewhere) by a pair of horns. His, however, are the horns, often understood to signify rays of celestial light, divinely acquired when the tables of the law were renewed on Mt. Sinai (Exodus 34).[25] Israelites at either side of their leader gaze at him with reverence and gratitude.

Curvature of the ivy and the frame of the miniature around the E *(Expliciunt)* indicate that the work of the scribe, as is customary, preceded decoration by the illuminator. Triple lines setting out the limits of the text were probably the first marks drawn on the page. The catchword *Kyrie* is repeated on the facing folio, where an illuminated initial introduces the Litany of the Saints.

LF 118. *Israelites Smitten by a Serpent*

Weary of their journey, the Israelites reproach God and Moses for having brought them out of Egypt, whereupon the Lord sends fiery serpents amongst them (Numbers 21:4–6). The miniature includes only one serpent, but he is of the highly efficient variety preferred by Belbello, and he is supervised in his work by an angel. In the monochromatic K *(Kyrie)*, a man clad only in transparent cloth seems to seek shelter from a menacing frond of acanthus.

In the lower border, the *biscia*, on a shield of silver leaf, is supported by angels whose knotted, flying scarves represent a second emblem of Filippo Maria, the *nodo* (see LF 85v). Radiant clouds complete the array of heraldry in one of the most elegant displays of armorials in the manuscript.

Et perdes omnes qui tribulant animã
meam quoniam ego seruus tuus sum.
Gloria patri et filio et spiritui sancto.
Sicut erat in principio et nunc et semp.
et in secula seculorum amen. antiphona.
Ne reminiscaris domine delicta mea ul'
parentum meorum neq; uindictam su
mas de peccatis meis.

Expliciunt septem psalmi penitenciales.

Incipiunt letanie sanctorum.

Incipiunt letanie sanctorum.

KYRIELEISON

rie leyson. Kyrie leyson.
pe audi nos. pe exaudi nos.
ater de celis deus misere nobis.

Eus in ad
iutorium
meum inte
de. Domi
ne ad adiuua
dum me festina. Confundantur et
reuereantur qui querunt animam.
Auertantur retrorsum et erubescant q
uolunt michi mala.
Auertantur statim et erubescentes q
dicunt michi euge euge.
Exultent et letentur inte omnes qque
runt te et dicant semper magnificetur do
minus qui dilligunt salutare tuum.
Ego uero egenus et pauper sum deus
adiuua me.

LF 123v.   *The Brazen Serpent*

The initial introduces Psalm LXIX in the Litany of the Saints. The Psalm, which begins, "O God, come to my assistance; O Lord, make haste to help me," is suitably illustrated by a miniature of Israelites appealing to the brazen serpent erected by Moses in order to heal victims of the fiery serpents (Numbers 21:7–9). The curative power of the brazen serpent made it a symbol of redemption in Christian theology and art, where it is often represented in connection with the Crucifixion. In Milan this symbol is especially significant, because a bronze believed to be the original brazen serpent has stood, probably since the early eleventh century, on a column in the basilica of Sant' Ambrogio. Unlike the relic, the serpent in the miniature is winged and lacks a loop in his body. The loop always occurs, however, in the *biscia*, which the Visconti may have adopted as an emblem because of the presence in their city of the sacred treasure.[26]

Partially nude figures seated in the framework of the initial point toward the brazen serpent. Although their gestures resemble those of the supplicants, these figures, like their predecessor on LF 118, emphasize the intensity of the drama without actually participating in it.

Requiem eternam dona eis domine. R̂.
Requiescant in pace. R̂. Amen. V̂.
Oremus pro fratribus nostris abscentibus R̂.
Saluos fac seruos tuos deus meus spe-
rantes in te. R̂.
Mitte eis domine auxilium de sancto.
R̂. Et desyon tuere eos. R̂.
Domine exaudi orationem meam. R̂.
Et clamor meus ad te veniat.
Oremus. Oratio.

Deus qui proprium
est misereri semp
[et] parcere suscipe de
precationem nostram.

mos et omnes famulos tuos quos delicto
rum catena constringit tue miseratio [et]
pietatis absoluat. Oratio.

LF 124v. *Balaam Opposed by an Angel*

The prophet Balaam was summoned by Balak, King of Moab, to curse the people of Israel. In the miniature, the prophet is shown en route to the Moabite kingdom. He is astounded, however, by the appearance of a glowering angel who threatens him with a drawn sword (Numbers 22:31). Balaam's donkey, first to perceive the angel, had refused to proceed against it. In his right hand, the prophet holds the whip with which he had beaten the loyal beast for its obstinacy. The confrontation occurs in a black and gold setting familiar from LF 89.

The D *(Deus)* introduces a prayer in the Litany. Embellished with pseudo-script, the initial terminates in a flourish of acanthus. The borders are exceptionally ornate, and all components of the page, including initials, line-endings, and even the rubrics, are part of a decorative pattern.

LF 126v.   *Balak Receives Balaam*

Permitted by the angel to complete his journey (see LF 124v), the prophet is received by the Moabite ruler (Numbers 22:36). Balaam's ample cloak sweeps over a ledge in the foreground of the miniature. His wiry, gold-lighted hair, curling beneath the brim of a sombrero, contrasts with the softer, white locks of his impressive host. The illuminator may have been unwilling to portray even an evil king as ugly; with regard to the monarch's attendants, however, he appears to have felt no such compunction. A colorful palace in the background reinforces the composition of the figures.

LF 127.   *Balaam Speaks with God*

Three times Balak commands Balaam to prepare holy sacrifices and then to curse the Israelites. In each instance Balaam makes a burnt offering, but he is constrained by the Lord to bless rather than curse Israel and to prophesy good things in its behalf (Numbers 23, 24). Although the biblical text places all three sacrifices on mountaintops, the Visconti illuminator portrays instead a three-aisled church terminating in a curved apse and surmounted by a polygonal dome. Two sheep burn on a furnace-like altar, before which Balaam kneels, communicating with a Deity not shown in the miniature. Identical bouquets of gold-centered roses form a geometric yet delicate frame.

LF 127v. *Balaam Blesses Israel*

His dignity now enhanced by flowing white hair, the prophet gives his blessing in a church which resembles Pharaoh's palace on LF 90v. The structure is modified for ecclesiastical use by the addition of a rose window on the facade and a cross atop the cupola above the apse of the building. A draped altar stands in the apse, surmounted by an altarpiece portraying saints. The group of Israelites being blessed also is derived from an earlier pattern in the manuscript, Joseph's family receiving his blessing on LF 79v. Although the later miniature lacks the delicacy of its formal predecessors, it is nonetheless distinguished by boldness of design and brilliance of color, especially in the gold-streaked raiment of the prophet and the glowing mantle of the Israelite in the foreground. In the borders, the Visconti motto, *a bon droyt*, is legible, though extensively worn, on a frame of silver bands. Lavish sprays of ivy complement the frothy gold design in the black background of the miniature.

LF 128. *Moses Sees the Promised Land*

(HOURS OF THE HOLY GHOST. MATINS)

Swathed in gold against a dramatic black sky, the Deity shows Moses the promised land to which the patriarch has led the Israelites, but which he himself will not be allowed to enter (Deuteronomy 34:1–4). Moses is soon to die at the age of one hundred twenty years. He still carries his miraculous rod, with which he points to a splendid, gold-capped city. Foliate sprays lacing its walls recall similar branches adorning the sheep in Belbello's first important contribution to the manuscript, the borders of LF 11. Leaves emerging from the cloud which encloses the miniature frame a thick-lipped, heavy face similar to the portrait in the lower right border of LF 57v. The borders are punctuated by smaller clouds framing the *biscia*. Scrolls curling around the frame once again display the Visconti motto. The small design preceding the rubric, for which burnished gold was probably intended (compare LF 118), was left incomplete.

Incipit officium de spiritu sancto. Ad
matutinum. Versus :—

DMNE LABIA

mea apries. R ⸹ Et os meum

annuntiabit laudem tuam. Versus.

LF 128v.   *Death of Moses*

As in the preceding miniature, Moses is hooded in yellow, but now his lined face is ashen, its modeling conspicuously unrelieved by red. Among the mourners, a young man at the foot of the bed is derived from the same pattern as Jacob on LF 74v. Adaptation from a model probably accounts for the incorrect proportioning of this figure, awkwardly perched on a bench which overlaps the edge of the pavement. The miniature recalls also the *Death of the Virgin* on LF 37. The patriarch, like the Virgin, lies on a gold-draped couch in a room with doors at either side. An image of the Madonna and Child on an altar behind Moses replaces the motif of the Lord caressing the Virgin's soul at the center of the earlier composition. Even the colors of the dragon in the lower border of LF 37 are transposed to the margins of the later folio. Towers once more appear at the sides. There is a great difference, however, between the fragile structures designed and perhaps even painted by the dei Grassi and the massive constructions which they inspired.

Moses' sanctity is emphasized by the presence of numerous angels on the page representing his death. Some dominate a cloister in the lower border; others cling to the branch which frames the miniature; and still two more, surprisingly bare, climb ladders toward companions overlooking a parapet.

The initial introduces the second verse of Matins in the Hours of the Holy Ghost.

Ad primam versus

tozum meum intende. R) Domne

ad adiuuandum me festina. Gloria

LF 129v.   *Spies before Jericho*

Appointed by the Lord to succeed Moses and lead the Israelites into the promised land, Joshua sends two spies to Jericho (Joshua 2:1). In the miniature, the bolder spy places his right hand, which holds a walking stick, on the hat of his skeptical companion, urging him to approach the drawbridge and the open gate of the city.

Accompanying the motto wound about the initial, emblems of the Comte de Vertus, adopted here by his son, appear in the borders. (Filippo Maria used the emblems even though the County of Vertus was inherited by his half-sister Valentina.) Three of the Virtues are identified by attributes familiar from earlier pages in the manuscript: Prudence holds a compass and sees her reflection in a mirror; Justice bears a sword in one hand and scales in the other; and Fortitude, wearing a lionskin tied over her head, is armed with a shield and stave. In the right border, Temperance holds an attribute new to her in the Visconti Hours but found also in other Italian representations, a sheathed sword turned downward, in contrast here to the upturned sword, also sheathed, of Justice.[27] (Pigment marring the figure of Temperance has rubbed off from the margin of the facing folio.) The Virtues are shown triumphant over Vices not specifically identified here by attributes. All are depicted as men, although in other representations their sex varies.

EUSINHOU
toríum meum íntende. R. Domíne
ad adíuuandum me festína. Glona

LF 130v. *Spies of Jericho Hidden*

Knowing that the Lord intends to give Jericho to the Israelites, the harlot Rahab hides Joshua's spies from soldiers sent in pursuit of them by her king. Still holding their staffs, the spies crouch in terror, as Rahab, her toe curling through the carding device propped against her body, prepares to conceal them with flax (Joshua 2:6). Outside the harlot's house (its roof adorned with gold grapevines), one of two helmeted soldiers listens attentively, while his companion, rapping at the door, peers through a crack to see who is within. Suspended from the waist of one of the soldiers is a scimitar, which, like the simulated arabic script on their garments, imparts an Oriental flavor to the proceedings. In the framework of the initial, Belbello introduces the horn motif which persists through the next miniature, culminating in the great blast of trumpets that brings down the walls of the city (LF 132v).

A reminder of the peacocks which adorned the Visconti gardens, four impressive specimens frame the page. The birds' bodies are modeled in a variety of rich colors, and a golden flame of feathers encloses each eye of their tails. In the upper and lower borders, the peacocks stand on strips of gold land so highly burnished that they suggest mirrors before which the birds may preen.

LF 131v. *Spies of Jericho Escape*

Rahab warily lets the spies down over the city wall with a rope (Joshua 2:15). Fastened to the twine is a plank which the men straddle during their descent. They have dropped their walking staffs in advance, and one of the two carries the traveling bag and hat worn also on their arrival (LF 129v). Extremely bold is the elaborate shadow cast on the wall at the left by the figures, their rope and plank, and even one of the staffs, whose shadow continues over the blue base of the wall onto the grass. At the sides of the initial, three angels blow trumpets. The smallest of the three blows the longest instrument, from which a Visconti pennant is suspended.

In the borders, birds of prey, some of them hooded, are tethered by long red cords which carry out the rope theme of the miniature. Standing on perches as brilliant as the foil provided for the peacocks which precede them, the hunting birds, like their predecessors, bespeak a personal interest of the Visconti. Three of the birds in the upper margin have lost parts of their heads through trimming.

Ad Nonam. Versus.

EIUSINAO

torum meum intende. omine

ad aduuandum me festina. Gloria

LF 132v.   *Conquest of Jericho*

(HOURS OF THE HOLY GHOST. NONE)

Jericho succumbs to a procession of Israelites. Trumpeters precede the ark of the covenant, transformed by the Christian artist to a large ciborium carried by a priest. The form of the container is echoed by numerous turrets within the city, illuminated, like the black sky, by a blaze which has toppled some of the towers. Fire has also breached the city wall, whose crenellations have begun to fall.

Visconti shields appear in apertures of the initial and in the borders. Those in corner quatrefoils are framed by suns painted on gold leaf.

LF 133v. *Sin of Achan*

Disobeying the divine command that the treasures of Jericho be anathema to the Israelites, Achan steals out of the ruined city, carrying a "golden rule of fifty sicles" and other loot in a sack on his shoulder (Joshua 7:21). Haloed figures stand beneath gables, at the sides of the D *(Deus)*. The long beard and sword of the man at the left are attributes of St. Paul, though the turban worn by this figure normally characterizes prophets rather than apostles. The tonsure and physiognomy of his counterpart are typical of St. Peter. Both Peter and Paul commonly hold books. The unpainted object (a cross?) at the right of the tessellated background may have been planned as an attribute of the tonsured figure. (The strut supporting the gable at the left is also unfinished.) Inasmuch as Christ's monogram appears in the following initial (LF 134v), a representation of two of his principal apostles may have been intended here.

A metallic display of armorials in the borders includes Visconti helmets and shields held by arms which sprout from foliage in the corners. Unpainted rays around the foliate forms suggest that the designer may have planned them as clouds. Lacquered scrolls on which the family motto is inscribed frame burnished suns whose rays alternate with additional scrolls. Some of the ivy sprays, in the lower right margins, are adorned by circles filled with red. Others are embellished by empty circles, and still others (in the left border) have no circles at all. The upper border has lost part of its decoration through trimming.

Ad complectoriu. ver

...torium meum intende. ℞. ...omine
ad adiuuandum me festina. Gloria

LF 134v. *Stoning of Achan*

Achan's transgression is discovered, and to appease their wrathful Deity the Israelites destroy the offender (Joshua 7:19–26). The punishment is depicted in two miniatures. In the first, Achan, tied to a column, is stoned by three of his compatriots. Their leader wears a high-crowned hat studded with pearls. His tunic and leggings respond to the vehemence of his hurling gesture. Beneath him, an assistant supports a basket heaped with additional stones. A third Israelite has collected his missiles in a fold of his tunic.

Christ's monogram appears in green on Visconti suns which seem to pierce the initial. Scroll-bearing doves alternate with vipers in the borders.

LF 136. *Burning of Achan, His Family, and His Possessions*

His face taut with anguish, Achan prays, as he, his family, and his flocks are consumed by fire. His wife gestures helplessly with her right hand; with the other, she gently touches the hand of one of her children.

The motto-bearing ribbon that winds around the D *(Domine)* is borrowed from LF 129v. The initial introduces the Hours of the Passion, rubricated on LF 135v.

OMINE LABIA

mea aperies. Ꝝ. Et os meum annun-

tiabit laudem tuam. Versus:

LF 136v. *Joshua Stops the Sun*

Joshua interrupts the course of the sun and the moon, thereby prolonging the day and allowing Israel sufficient time to destroy the armies of five kings who had attacked her allies, the Gibeonites (Joshua 10:12–14). Normally clothed as a warrior in this scene, Joshua is instead depicted here as a patriarch. He wears a sweeping mauve mantle highlighted in yellow over a blue tunic streaked with gold. White in his shawl and on the upturned brim of his hat adds prominence to his swarthy face and jutting beard. His pointing gesture is emphasized by the opposing attitudes of two enemy soldiers: one prepares to hurl a lance from the battlements, while the second, stepping through the gate, aims his weapon at an Israelite who threatens him with a metallic weight. Behind this Hebrew soldier, whose greaves protect a pair of parti-colored hose, stands a third member of the enemy force, identified by the scorpion on his shield. Helmets, lances, and two pairs of gleaming white eyes hint at the numbers of the enemy host within the fortress. Careful attention to the equipment of the warriors here and elsewhere in the Visconti Hours is not surprising in a manuscript made for the ruler of Milan, a city long renowned for its production of arms and armor.

In accordance with the text, representations of the event depicted on this folio traditionally include the moon as well as the sun. In the Visconti miniature, however, the moon is absent. Although other stars appear, the sun at its zenith dominates the sky. The emblematic significance of this sun, whose pinwheel effect is enhanced by a kind of pivot at its center, is accentuated by the Visconti tilting helmets which flank it at either side of the initial. Red glazing of the sphere atop the helmet at the right, unusual for Belbello, is a reminder of the dei Grassi portion of the manuscript.

The D *(Deus)* introduces the second verse of Matins in the Hours of the Passion.

LF 142. *Ehud Presents a Gift to Eglon*

(HOURS OF THE PASSION. LAUDS)

Ehud, the second of the judges who governed Israel after the death of Joshua, was chosen by the Lord to assassinate Eglon, king of the Moabites, who had oppressed the Hebrews for eighteen years (Judges 3:14–25). Ehud's destruction of Eglon unfolds leisurely in the Visconti Hours, where it is described in two miniatures. In the first, the Israelite kneels before the king, offering him a veiled gift. Ehud's head, which duplicates Joshua's from the preceding miniature, is made even more pugnacious by a protruding lower lip. The king and his attendants display surprise, verging on suspicion, at the homage rendered by an enemy. Like King Balak on LF 126v, Eglon wears a crown over an imposing headdress. The upturned hem of his mantle discloses a mauve tunic bordered with pseudo-script, which also decorates bands within the text. He is armed with a bow on one side and a scimitar on the other. A golden tree and white flowers within the walls perhaps allude to the "summer parlour" in which, according to the text, the murder will take place. Heavy leaves frame the miniature and recur in the borders, where unpainted lines around them again suggest that radiant suns or clouds may have been originally intended (see also LF 133v).

LF 144v. *Ehud Kills Eglon*

(HOURS OF THE PASSION. PRIME)

Having duped Eglon into dismissing his attendants, Ehud stabs him in the abdomen with a dagger. Neither his bow and quiver nor his heavily laden purse has availed the king against the wrath of God. Powerful shoulders suggest the strength of the assassin, whose short tunic also reveals a pair of well-formed legs. Ivy and floral rinceaux enclosing Visconti shields frame the miniature as well as the page. A large tri-colored spray links the D *(Deus)* with exceptionally wide gold bands in the borders.

LF 146. *Jael Kills Sisera*

(HOURS OF THE PASSION. TERCE)

Still another enemy of Israel is vanquished on this folio. Having welcomed and offered milk to the Canaanite general Sisera, the Israelite woman Jael kills him by driving a nail of the tent through his head (Judges 4:21). Exertion has loosened strands of the heroine's hair. Normally she is shown bending over the sleeping general to commit the murder, but Belbello's miniature (structurally similar to the shearing of Samson on LF 155v) is a much more explicit representation of pride brought low by humility. The radiant initial terminates in a sun framing the Visconti dove. Delicate arabesques behind the initial and in the borders are appropriate to the feminine theme.

ullos usq; ineternum. Persingulos
dies benedicimus te. Et laudabilis
nomen tuum ineternum et inseculum
seculi. Dignare domine dieisto. Sine peccato nos custodire. Miserere nri
domine miserere nri. Fiat misericordia tua domine super nos. quemadmo-
dum speravimus inte. Inte domine
speravi. non confundar ineternum. Ad lau-
des antha. Per signum crucisdum-
mcas nostris libera nos deus noster.
Eus inadiuto-
rium meu in-
tende. Domine
ad adiuuandum

costraho

to:uum meum intende. W. Domine

ad adiuuandum me festina. Gloria

ut uisione tua ubiqʒ armati. ꝫ hostes uin
cere. ꝫ ad tua ueleamus gloriam peruenire.
Q ui uuus ꝫ regnas cum deo patre in unita
spu sancti deus per omnia secula seculoru.
R. Amen. R. Domine exaudi
orationem meam. R. Et clamor me
us ad te ueniat. V. Benedicam domin
co gratias. Ad terciam. antipha.
Per signum crucis de inimicis nostris libe
ra nos deus noster. Versus.

Eus in ad

iutorium

meum in

tende.

Domine

ad adiuuan

obtulisti. fac nos quesumus sic penitenc
crucem portare. ut in extremo iudicio per
te pium iudicem eterne mortis sententia
fugiamus. Qui unus regnas. ꝛc. ꝟ.
Domine exaudi orationem meam. ꝶ
Et clamor meus ad te veniat. ꝟ
Benedicamus domino. ꝶ Deo gra
tias. Ad sextam ant. Per signum
crucis de inimicis nostris libera nos deus nr. ꝟ.

eius in ad
iutorium
meum in
tende.
Domi
ne ad adiu

LF 147v.   *Jephthah Sacrifices His Daughter*

Continuing the series of murders is the ritual sacrifice of a victim who, unlike her predecessors, is innocent. Jephthah, the Israelite leader, fulfills his vow that if his people are granted victory over the Ammonites he will offer as a holocaust whatever he first sees upon his return to his home (Judges 11:30–40). Heavy-lidded, the father holds his bloodstained dagger poised to strike his wounded daughter again. The golden-haired virgin reassures her father that he must keep his promise to the Lord. The blazing altar, completing a triad of colors that includes also Jephthah's green mantle and his daughter's blue robe, resembles the grill on which Abraham prepares to sacrifice Isaac (LF 74). The two events are, of course, also analogous in prefiguring the sacrifice of Christ by his Father. Lettered in gold on either side of the initial is the Visconti motto.

LF 149.   *Samson Slays a Lion*

Samson is represented in the Visconti Hours by nine narrative scenes, more than the number devoted to any other Old Testament figure except Moses. His prominence in Filippo Maria's manuscript can probably be explained in part by his attractiveness to the worldly prince as a paradigm of God-given power. In addition, however, Samson was theologically significant as a forerunner of Christ. His suffering and ultimate triumph through death prefigured the passion and resurrection of the Savior. Finally, to the artist, the hero's exploits presented inviting possibilities for illustration. (The importance of Samson's hair must have been especially welcome to Belbello: rarely elsewhere are his flowing tresses portrayed with such enthusiasm.)

The opening miniature in the Visconti Samson cycle illustrates the first of his miraculous accomplishments, the slaying of a lion with his bare hands (Judges 14:6). In accordance with a widespread pictorial convention, Samson straddles the lion (or seems to—both man and beast are more successful decoratively than anatomically) and rends its jaws from behind. Framing the miniature is a chain of circular forms linked by four-petaled pink and blue blossoms which reappear in gold emulsion within the rings. Cloth draped over the stem of the D (*Deus*) provides the flourish which completes it.

cens crucem ascendisti. in qua durissimis
clauis affixus et inter latrones ductus:
pependisti. 7 peccatoribz inlatronem spem
de uenia tribuisti. Presta ut te crucifixum
incorde semp habentes. 9tia omnium pec-
catoꝛ nꝛe facila uirtute tuoꝛ uulneriꝰ
sentiamus. Qui uiuis regnas. ꝛc. ꝛ.
Domine exaudi orationem meã. ꝛ.
Et clamoꝛ meus ad te ueniat ꝟ. Bñ
dicam̃ dñõ. ꝛ. Deo gꝛãs. Ad nona. ant.
Per signũ crucis de inimicis nris libera
nos deus noster. Versus.

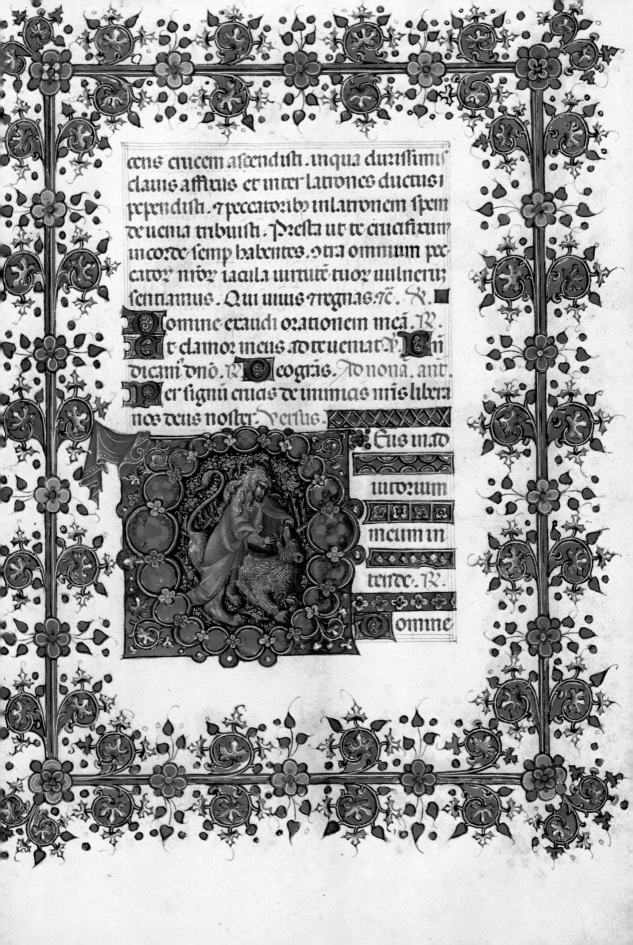

Eus in ad

iutoꝛium

meum in

tende. ꝛ.

Domine

mans spiritū emisisti. Et ad limbum descenden
ut captiuos educeres portas 7 uectes infor
titudine 7 virgulti passionis tue virtute. con
cede ut in hora mortis peccatorum carceris
9 fractis 7 hostes uincere. 7 ad tua meriti
gaudia peruenire. Qui uiuis. ꝛ̃. Ꝟ.
ominē exaudi orationem meam. Ꝝ.
t clamor meus ad te ueniat. Ꝟ.
ñdicamus domino. Ꝝ. eo gra
tias. Ad uesperas antħa.
er signum crucis de inimicis nris libe
ra nos deus noster. Versus.

eus in ad
iutorium
meum in
tende. Ꝝ.
omine

LF 150v. *Samson Slays Philistines*

Armed only with the jawbone of an ass, Samson destroys an enemy force whose military equipment far surpasses his. The hero now wears a double-pointed beard in addition to the uncut hair which is the source of his prowess. Astride a victim whose left leg has buckled (and whose shield is emblazoned with the evil scorpion), he prepares to strike two opponents who threaten him with swords; simultaneously, he thrusts back still another astounded adversary. The circular form and the colors of the initial reappear in Visconti emblems and roseate blossoms in the borders. An abundance of burnished leaf in the margins augments the ember-like glow of gold emulsion in the miniature.

Inasmuch as the miniature precedes the episode of foxes with firebrands (Judges 15:4–5), it should refer to Samson's slaying of thirty Philistines in Judges 14:19. The jawbone, however, occurs only in a subsequent moment of the story, Samson's destruction of a thousand Philistines in Judges 15:15. This slight departure from narrative sequence—the only deviation of its kind in the manuscript—suggests that at some point in the history of the illustration of the Samson cycle, Belbello or a predecessor, using a full pictorial model containing both scenes of combat, transposed to the first incident the famous weapon textually appropriate to the second.

LF 153.   *Foxes with Firebrands*

(HOURS OF THE PASSION. COMPLINE)

Wearing the sweeping blue mantle familiar from the opening miniature of the cycle, Samson releases foxes with flaming tails into the corn fields of the Philistines (Judges 15:4–5). Golden grain, ignited by three of the animals in its midst, glows against a dense landscape which gives the illusion of having been cut into the burnished gold leaf that surrounds it. Sprays of intense red, mauve, blue, and turquoise blossoms resembling sweet peas frame the page.

Small initials above and below the principal letter enclose representations of the Deity.

libera nos deus noster. Versus.

Onuent nos deus salutaris no
ster. R. Et auerte iram ti
am a nobis. Versus.

Eus ui ad

iutorium

meum in

tende. R.

Domine

ad adiuuan

dum me festina. Gloria patri. ꝛc. ant.
Tullit yoseph corpus ihesu et inuol
uit illud in syndone munda et posuit il
lud in monumento. psalmus.
Laudate dominum in sanctis

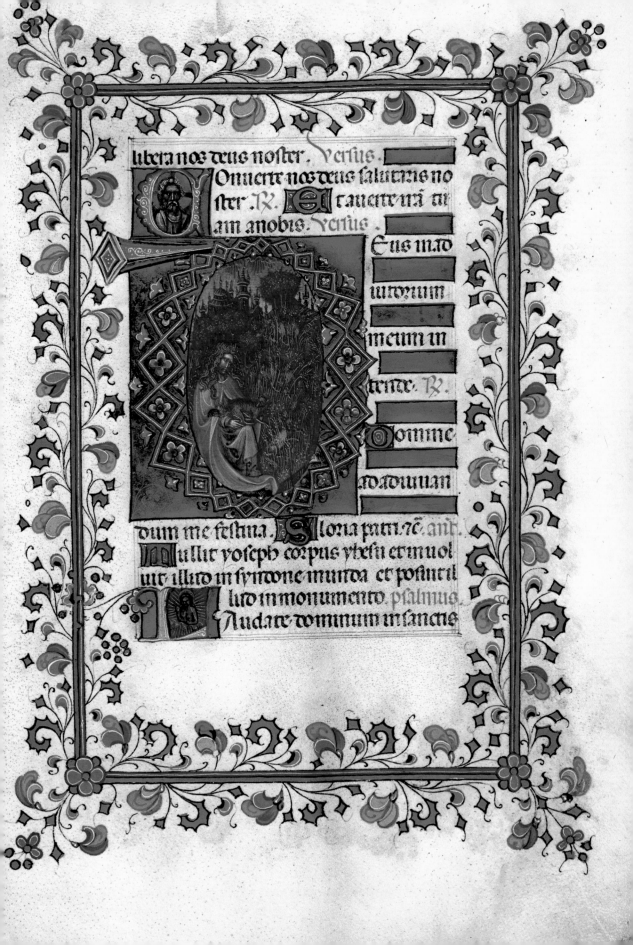

LF 155.   *The Gates of Gaza*

Samson confounds the enemies who had planned to trap and kill him in their city by removing its gates, complete with bolt and hinges, and carrying them on his shoulder to the top of a hill (Judges 16:3). Astonished observers in the foreground of the miniature include, at the left, a delicately modeled figure with a corn-silk beard and, at the right, the thwarted Philistines, two of them holding arrows.

The motif of the burdened hero climbing a hill suggests Christ's ascent of Calvary, and the palm tree which echoes Samson's colossal figure reinforces the implication of victory through martyrdom. The landscape also includes several vignettes of country life: sheep graze beneath a fruit tree; above them a hound pursues a stag; and still higher a herdsman or hunter winds his horn. Schematic rays emanating from the sky do not themselves brighten the scene below. Gold which pervades the miniature, however, like the *couleur changeante* of the draperies, attests to the illuminator's interest in actual effects of light.

In the borders, silvery Visconti shields are set against burnished gold bands adorned by sprays of berries and roses.

LF 155 v. *Delilah Betrays Samson*

As he lies sleeping in her lap, Delilah shears Samson's strength-giving locks (Judges 16:19). Seated on a green cushion and swathed in glowing mauve and red drapery, the seductress wears a gold-flecked magenta toque over her own scraggly hair. Three Philistines lurk behind her, waiting to take Samson prisoner. The interior of Delilah's house contains several spaces, ingeniously suggested by partitions, ceiling beams, and a foliated column. In the alcove at the rear is a platform bed. The exterior of the structure is enhanced by a curious selection of abundantly detailed architectural features, including turrets, a porch with stairs, a balcony, a loggia, and an ogival canopy. Bouquets of glittering phlox-like flowers compose a frame in the borders.

LF 156 v. *Samson Taken Prisoner*

(HOURS OF THE CROSS. MATINS)

A closely shorn Samson struggles in vain against the brutish captor whose longer hair emphasizes his strength, now greater than his victim's. Representations of this episode as a separate scene following Samson's betrayal by Delilah are rare even in full cycles of his life. The position of the miniature in the Visconti Hours, however, as well as elements of its iconography, suggests an intended parallel with the Taking of Christ in the Garden of Gethsemane, a subject which frequently introduces the office begun on this page. A throng of soldiers holding weapons arrayed against the sky is traditional in the Christian scene, and the conspicuously unhelmeted, white-bearded figure amidst Samson's tormentors recalls Peter, who commonly turns aside to cut off the ear of a soldier in depictions of the capture of Christ. In the flowered meadow which frames the initial are six striking nudes whose relationship to the scene within is puzzling.

Visconti armorials in the borders include the *biscia* and blazing suns encircled by lacquered scrolls bearing the family motto, now worn. Rays drawn around the scrolls were left unpainted.

LF 157. *Samson Blinded*

Normally, Samson's tormentors blind him by thrusting a sharp object into his eyes. Here, however, the heavy-jowled Philistine of the facing miniature prepares to force the hero's head into a metal cauldron filled with burning coals.

Like the floral pattern behind the initial, the design of the borders also links this folio with the facing page. Corresponding to the suns on 156v are four kaleidoscopic medallions, one filled with oak-like foliage and the others with tracery suggesting rose windows. Crocketed gables in the lateral margins are related to architectural forms in the D *(Deus)*.

torium meum intende. R̃. Domine
ad adiuuandum me festina. Gloria

patri ⁊ filio. ⁊ spiritui sc̄o. Sicut erat
in principio ⁊ nunc ⁊ semp. ⁊ in secula se
culorum amen alla. ant. A doram⁹
te xp̄e ⁊ benedicimus tibi. hymnus.

Patris sapientia ue
ritas diuina. deus
homo captus est
hora matutina. a
notis discipulis. cito derelict.
a iudeis uenditus traditus et
afflictus. ant. A doramus
te xp̄e ⁊ benedicimus tibi. qa p
sanctam crucem tuam redemisti
mundum. ꝟ. Domine ⁊
exaudi orationem meam. ꝝ.
Et clamor meus ad te ueni
at. Oremus. oratio.

LF 157 v.   *The Lord Blessing*

A small miniature of God the Father blessing introduces a hymn which says that Christ was captured at the hour of Matins. In his left hand the Deity holds a golden orb. He looks toward two kneeling angels in the P *(Patris)*, who present Visconti tilting helmets. (Although the lower angel's back is to the Lord, he gazes nonetheless intently toward Him.) The initial is completed by a green ribbon embellished with the motto, *a bon droyt*, which recurs on blue and magenta bands in the borders. Throughout the page, as in many preceding folios, highly burnished gold irradiates Belbello's preferred combination of colors: deep red, blue, and green.

torium meum intende. R̃. Ō Domi

ne ad adiuuandum me festina. Glo

LF 158v. *Samson at the Mill*

After his capture and blinding, Samson is imprisoned in Gaza and forced to grind grain for the Philistines (Judges 16:21). Even more than the well on LF 78v, the mill, which almost fills a room, evinces the illuminator's interest in ingenious mechanical contrivances. Grain pours into the millstone from a woven container whose funneled end is tied open (particles scattered in the grinding process appear on the surface of the stone). Holding a lever stabilized by a long gold cord, Samson manipulates the shaft which turns the millstone. On the floor are two empty baskets, one perhaps used to bring grain to the mill, the other to scoop it in lighter amounts into the funnel.

Although Samson's hair is still short, his beard has grown back. He does not appear to be blind, but two reading hermits in the initial allude indirectly to the subject of sight. The rudimentary architecture which shelters these figures—platforms and simple gables supported by unplaned logs—evokes the primitive dwellings of the pious recluses who dwelt in the wilderness (see LF 30).

In the borders, slender but vibrant angels support enormous Visconti helmets. They also hold viper shields, which recur in the upper and lower margins within burnished gold quatrefoils adorned by punched rays.

LF 160. *Death of Samson*

Although Samson's blindness is more apparent here than in the preceding miniature, his long hair, now white, suggests that he has regained his strength. He destroys the temple of the Philistines, thereby bringing about his own death but at
the same time overcoming his enemies (Judges 16:30).

Angels standing in draped gold pavilions at the sides of the miniature hold
scepters and Visconti shields. Silver banners fly above the tents. Metallic pigments
are juxtaposed also in the borders, where silver shields and scrolls are set off by
burnished gold.

LF 161v. *Elkanah and His Family*

Biblical illustration of the Visconti Hours begins with a narrative of the birth and youth of the Virgin. It ends with the story of another child, Samuel, who was likewise divinely granted to a pious but barren woman and then dedicated by his parents to the service of the Lord. (The circumstances of Samson's birth, though not depicted in the manuscript, are also similar.) Samuel's miraculous birth and his early devotion to God are described in I Kings 1–3 (I Samuel 1–3 in versions other than the Douay).

In the opening miniature of the sequence, Samuel is not yet born. Hannah, still barren, is led to the temple by her husband Elkanah. They are accompanied also by Elkanah's second wife, Peninnah, who caresses the head of one of her numerous children; Elkanah, however, looks benignly not at them but at Hannah. The figures, like the verdant landscape around them, are painted with exceptional care. Hannah's hair glistens through a transparent wimple. The light which whitens her blue gown is expressed also by yellow strokes on the green and deep rose garments of Elkanah and his second wife. The figure of the husband is accented not only by his red mantle but also by the sweeping white brim of his hat, which, like Peninnah's shawl and the gesture of one of her sons, directs the observer's eye to the family's destination. The domed polygonal sanctuary which crowns the landscape contains an altar adorned by a retable. Behind the principal structure stands a bell tower.

Interlaced foliate and geometric forms constitute the initial. Its principal colors—rose, green, and gold—recur in the tessellated pattern behind it, in which each gold square is punched. Small white shields in the initial are complemented by larger Visconti emblems in the borders: radiant doves and scrolls. Four of the latter are held by red-sleeved arms, drastically abbreviated reminders of the angels who perform a similar function in the borders of LF 158v.

LF 163.   *Hannah Blessed by Eli*

(HOURS OF THE CROSS. NONE)

The priest Eli blesses Hannah and prays that the God of Israel will grant her a son (I Kings 1:17). Cool periwinkle blue lighted by yellow in Hannah's gown contrasts with the stronger hues of the priest's vestments. Two saints in the wings of the triptych on the green marble altar behind the figures venerate a third image, obscured by the priest, in its central panel. The Visconti motto remains only partially legible on scrolls which compose the initial.

The dove in the upper border is not simply a Visconti emblem. A halo identifies it as the Holy Spirit, whose presence in the context of the blessing of Hannah constitutes an appropriate allusion to the conception of Christ. Its counterpart in the lower margin is the Lamb of the Apocalypse, the resurrected Christ who alone was worthy to open the book with seven seals. Both Lamb and book have lost part of their pigment. Seraphim alternating with gold clouds glazed in red complete the array of celestial symbols.

LF 164v.   *Presentation of Samuel in the Temple*

(HOURS OF THE CROSS. VESPERS)

Hannah fulfills her vow to dedicate her son to the Lord (I Kings 1:28). With only slight modifications—most notably the introduction of the child on the altar—the composition of this miniature is a replica of its predecessor. The space of the second painting, however, is more compressed, its colors less luminous, and its broad-faced, thick-necked figures more sharply modeled and less elegant than their counterparts on LF 163. These differences probably disclose the intervention of an assistant in the second miniature.

Although Visconti armorials are lacking, the folio is rich in gold, which is hatched with black in the foliate initial and adorned by arabesques of multicolored leaves and flowers in the borders.

LF 166.   *Samuel Called by the Lord*

(HOURS OF THE CROSS. COMPLINE)

The radiant Lord appears amidst wisps of white clouds to awaken his faithful servant, fallen asleep before the altar, and endow him with prophetic power (I Kings 3: 2–14). Flying from one of the turrets in the C (*Converte*) is a pennant inscribed with the words *iustitia* and *forteza*. Personifications of these Cardinal Virtues, the last Visconti emblems in the manuscript, stand on gold pedestals in the borders. Each wears gold armor and a crown and holds a Visconti helmet. Justice is armed with a sword and Fortitude with a mace. A floral spray growing through the high wall of the initial complements the garden behind the Virtues.

torium meum intende. R. Domine

ad adiuuandum me festina. Glo

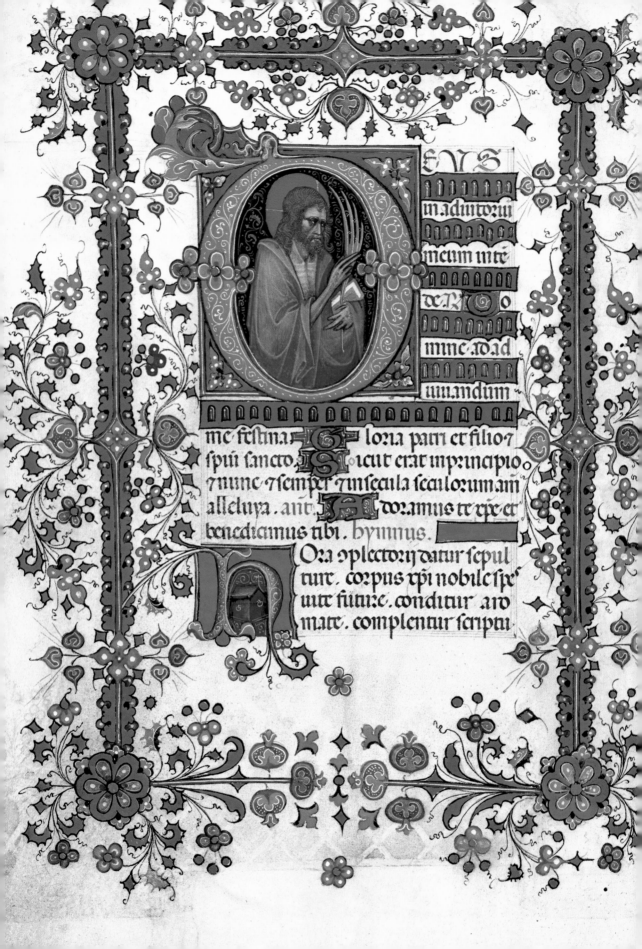

EVS
in adiutoriu
meum inte
De P.
mine ad ad
iuuandum
me festina. Gloria patri et filio 7
spui sancto. Sicut erat in principio
7 nunc 7 semper 7 in secula seculorum am
alleluya. ant. Adoramus te xpe et
benedicamus tibi. hymnus.

Ora oplectorij datur sepul
ture. corpus xpi nobile spe
uite future. conditur aro
mate. complentur scriptu

LF 166v.   *The Redeemer*

The final miniature in the Visconti Hours is an image of the Risen Christ. Covering his emaciated body is a mantle of regal purple. The yellow highlights of this robe, together with an abundance of gold in the halo, the hair, and even the brows of the Savior, enhance his otherworldly aspect. A red book in Christ's left arm emphasizes the color of the blood which seeps from his wounds. He also holds a palm whose form is echoed by the slender fingers of his blessing hand and whose color is restated in the initial which frames the representation. The Holy Sepulcher appears within a smaller initial beneath the Redeemer. Exuberant sprays of foliage and flowers in the borders celebrate his Resurrection.

Provenance and Format
of the Visconti Hours

BR 397. Acquired by the National Library in 1969 from Duke Uberto Visconti di Modrone. 151 leaves, trimmed, approximately 247 x 175 mm. Modern foliation in lower left corner. Extensive water stains, especially in upper borders. The gatherings are: 1–8, 9–16, 17–24, 25–32, 33–40, 41–48, 49–56, 57–64, 65–72, 73–80, 81–88, 89–96, 97–104, 105–112, 113–120, 121–128, 129–136, 137–144, 145–151 (the conjugate leaf of 147 is lacking). Catchwords and the sequence of the text indicate that the folios are in their original order.

LF 22. Acquired from Prince G. Rospigliosi in 1902 by Baron Horace Landau.

Given to Florence after the death of his great-nephew Baron Horace Finaly in 1945. 167 leaves, trimmed, approximately 250 x 179 mm. Modern foliation in lower right corner. The gatherings are: 1–8, 9–15 (13 is a single leaf), 16–23, 24–31, 32–39, 40–47, 48–55, 56–63, 64–71, 72–79, 80–87, 88–95, 96–103, 104–109, 110–117, 118–125, 126–127, 128–135, 136–143, 144–151, 152–155, 156–163, 164–167. The catchword *Deus* (the only catchword in red ink) on folio 135v precedes a prayer beginning with *Domine* on the facing folio. All other catchwords are correct, and the folios appear to be in their original order.

Related Manuscripts Discussed in the Text

Antwerp, Plantin-Moretus Museum, ms. 15. Bible of Konrad von Vechta.

Bergamo, Biblioteca Civica, ms. delta. 7.14. Sketchbook.

Chambéry, Bibliothèque municipale, ms. 4. Breviary of Marie of Savoy.

The Hague, Royal Library, ms. 76 F 6. Hours of Isabel of Castille.

London, British Museum, Add. 15277. Bible (Exodus through Joshua); additional books in Rovigo.

Mantua, Palazzo Ducale, Missal of Barbara of Brandenburg, Marchioness of Mantua.

Milan, Biblioteca Ambrosiana, ms. E.24 Inf. Pliny, *Natural History*.

Milan, Biblioteca Ambrosiana, ms. E.18 Inf. Missal.

Milan, Biblioteca Braidense, ms. AE.XIV. 19–20. *Acta Sanctorum*.

Milan, Biblioteca Trivulziana, lat. 2262. Breviary and Beroldo's treatise on Milanese liturgy.

Milan, S. Ambrogio, Chapter Library, ms. 6. Coronation Missal of Giangaleazzo Visconti.

Modena, Biblioteca Estense, ms. alfa. R.7. 3 (lat. 842). Book of Hours.

Munich, Bayerische Staatsbibliothek, lat. 23215. Hours of Blanche of Savoy.

Oxford, Bodleian Library, Digby 224. Livy, *Roman History*, First Decade.

Paris, Bibliothèque nationale, ital. 118, 119. Livy, *Roman History*, Third and Fourth Decades.

Paris, Bibliothèque nationale, ital. 131. Suetonius, *Lives of the Caesars*.

Paris, Bibliothèque nationale, lat. 757. Book of Hours and Missal.

Paris, Bibliothèque nationale, lat. 5888. Petrus de Castelleto, Funeral Oration for Giangaleazzo Visconti.

Paris, Bibliothèque nationale, lat. 8204. Virgil, *Aeneid*.

Paris, Bibliothèque nationale, nouv. acq. fr. 5243. *Giron le Courtois*.

Paris, Bibliothèque nationale, Smith–Lesouëf 22. Book of Hours and Missal.

Rome, Biblioteca Casanatense, ms. 459. *Historia Plantarum*.

Rome, Biblioteca Vaticana, Barb. lat. 613. *Bible historiale*.

Rovigo, Biblioteca dell'Accademia dei Concordi, ms. 212. Bible (Genesis and Ruth); additional books in London.

Vienna, National Library, ms. 2759–2764. Bible of King Wenceslaus.

Notes

Introduction Part I

1. For the documents on Giovannino and his collaborators, see Arslan, 1963, pp. 58–60.
2. See Toesca, *Pittura e miniatura*, 1912, fig. 225.
3. M. Magistretti, *Beroldus sive Ecclesiae Ambrosianae Ordines*, Milan, 1894, p. 51.
4. Arslan, 1963, p. 60; M. L. Gengaro and L. Arano Cogliati, *Miniature Lombarde*, 1970, pp. 50, 407.

Introduction Part II

5. For other Psalter-Hours of the fourteenth and fifteenth centuries, see V. Leroquais, *Les psautiers manuscrits des bibliothèques de France*, Macon, 1940–1941, I, p. LIXf. For the history and structure of Books of Hours see Leroquais, *Les livres d'heures manuscrits de la Bibliothèque nationale*, Paris, 1927, I, pp. I–LXXXV, and J. Plummer, *Liturgical Manuscripts for the Mass and the Divine Office*, New York, 1964, pp. 32, 45–51.
6. Professor Julian Brown, who has recently examined the manuscript, concurs with Toesca's judgment (1951, p. IV) that the script is uniform.
7. Dr. Filippo di Benedetto, Mr. Anthony Cains, and Mrs. Barbara Giuffrida made this examination when the manuscripts were unbound for photography in 1971.
8. Single or small groups of scenes from the life of the Virgin sometimes appear in pictorial narratives of the Bible preceding Psalters. A short cycle of the early life of the Virgin, including four episodes from her parents' life before her birth, occurs in the Book of Hours made for Giangaleazzo's mother, Blanche of Savoy (Munich, Staatsbibliothek, lat. 23215).
9. B. Corio, *L'historia di Milano*, Venice, 1554, p. 264f.
10. The marriage contract was published by E. Jarry, *La vie politique de Louis de France, duc d'Orléans, 1372–1407*, Paris, 1889, pp. 392–406.
11. C. Magenta, *I Visconti e gli Sforza nel Castello di Pavia*, Milan, 1883, I, pt. 1, p. 183.
12. Vienna, Nationalbibliothek, ms. 2759–2764 (Bible of King Wenceslaus) and Antwerp, Plantin-Moretus Museum, ms. 15 (Bible of Konrad von Vechta). See M. Frinta, "The Master of the Gerona Martyrology and Bohemian Illumination," *Art Bulletin*, XLVI, 1964, pp. 283–289; J. von Schlosser, "Die Bilderhandschriften König Wenzels," *Jahrbuch der Kunsthistorischen Sammlungen des Allerhöchsten Kaiserhauses*, XIV, 1893, pp. 214–317; G. Schmidt, "Malerei bis 1450," in *Gotik in Böhmen*, Munich, 1969, pp. 231–237, 247ff.
13. The Books of Genesis and Ruth are in Rovigo, Bibl. dell'Accademia dei Concordi, ms. 212. Exodus, Numbers, Leviticus, Deuteronomy, and Joshua are in London, Brit. Mus., Add. 15277. See G. Folena and G. L. Mellini, *Bibbia istoriata padovana della fine del Trecento*, Venice, 1962.
14. Toesca, 1912, pp. 536ff., 582. The correspondence was published by F. Carta, *Codici, corali e libri a stampa miniati della Biblioteca Nazionale di Milano*, Rome, 1891, p. 153ff.
15. The Visconti and Sforza library has been studied and its inventories published by E. Pellegrin, *La bibliothèque des Visconti et des Sforza ducs de Milan, au XVe siecle*, Paris, 1955; Supplement, Florence, 1969.
16. I plan to return to this problem in a subsequent publication. I am grateful to the Samuel H. Kress Foundation for the fellowship that has enabled me to continue my study of the manuscript.

Commentaries

All biblical citations are from the Douay version. Proper names, however, are given in the more familiar forms of the King James Bible.

1. For a history of apocryphal accounts of the life of the Virgin and their reflection in the visual arts, see J. Lafontaine-Dosogne, *Iconographie de l'enfance de la Vierge dans l'Empire Byzantin et en Occident*, Brussels, 1964–1965, 2v.

2. Although children are sometimes present in representations of the Marriage of the Virgin, from which the composition of the Marriage of Anna and Joachim is derived (see, for example, BR 90, which does not, however, include children), the boy and girl on BR 1 may refer to Giangaleazzo's son and daughter by his first marriage: Azzone (who died in 1381) and Valentina were eleven and ten years old when their father remarried.

3. The date near the base of the temple is discussed in Part I of the Introduction.

4. For Professor Meiss's discussion of Giovannino's use of gold, see the Introduction, Part I, and *French Painting in the Time of Jean de Berry*, 1967, p. 143.

5. Panel by Turone in Brussels, Musée Royal (E. Sandberg-Vavalà, "A Chapter in Fourteenth Century Iconography: Verona," *Art Bulletin*, XI, 1929, pp. 376–412, fig. 2).

6. The watchful cheetah is a small replica of its counterpart on folio 1 of the Bergamo sketchbook. Tethered cheetahs appear also among a series of family and personal emblems in the Missal illuminated for Giangaleazzo when he was made Duke of Milan in 1395 (Milan, S. Ambrogio, Chapter Library, ms. 6, fol. 8). In Africa and Asia these animals were trained to run down game. It is possible that they were used for this purpose also by the Visconti, renowned for their interest in hunting and for the innumerable hunting animals and prey kept in their park at Pavia (Magenta, I, pt. 1, pp. 119ff., 341f.).

7. This passage from Voragine's *Golden Legend*, as well as those which follow, are from the edition of G. Ryan and H. Ripperger, New York, 1941. The narrative of the Virgin's youth in the reading for September 8 concludes with the Annunciation.

8. Arslan, 1963, p. 61f. See also M. Harrsen, "Figural Grisaille Ornament on a Historiated Initial of about 1400, and the Derivation of this Style from the Indulgences of Avignon," in *Bookmen's Holiday* (essays in honor of H. M. Lydenberg), ed. D. Fulton, New York, 1943, pp. 316–322.

9. Acanthus and oak foliage appear in the Visconti Hours with frequency and in contexts which suggest an emblematic meaning. Acanthus, however, is widely prevalent in other manuscripts of the period not associated with the Visconti.

Oak leaves and trees are depicted throughout the Visconti prayer book with varying degrees of realism; occasionally they are accompanied by acorns (BR 2v, 145, LF 17). Portraits in the pictorial genealogy of the Visconti painted ca. 1403 by Michelino da Besozzo in the illuminated eulogy of Giangaleazzo (Paris, Bibl. nat., lat. 5888, fols. 7–12v) are framed by branches of oak leaves with acorns.

10. For the motif of the Child in the Annunciation, its derivation from the *Lignum vitae* of Bonaventura and its origin in early fourteenth-century Tuscan painting, see D. Robb, "The Iconography of the Annunciation in the Fourteenth and Fifteenth Centuries," *Art Bulletin*, XVIII, 1936, pp. 523–526.

11. *Meditations on the Life of Christ*, ed. I. Ragusa and R. B. Green, Princeton, 1961, p. 24f. In a Lombard Missal and Book of Hours related to the Visconti Hours and datable ca. 1380, the Virgin is depicted swaddling the newborn Baptist (Paris, Bibl. nat., lat. 757, fol. 337v). As in the Visconti miniature, the child points and wears a hair shirt. Women playing catch amidst acanthus appear in initials of the same manuscript (fols. 404, 406v).

For the iconography of the Infant St. John, see M. A. Lavin, "Giovannino Battista: A Study in Renaissance Religious Symbolism," *Art Bulletin*, XXXVII, 1955, pp. 85–101, and "Giovannino Battista: A Supplement," *Art Bulletin*, XLIII, 1961, pp. 319–326.

12. For a recent survey of the history of the legend of *Ara Coeli* and its representations in medieval art, see Meiss, 1967, pp. 233–235.

13. The *Ara Coeli* and the *Magi Seeing a Star* appear in the wings of Roger van der Weyden's Bladelin Altarpiece, now in Berlin, painted ca. 1452, after his return from Italy (E. Panofsky, *Early Netherlandish Painting*, Cambridge [Mass.], 1953, II, figs. 336–338). The *Nativity* in the central panel of the altarpiece includes both the radiant child and the column which occur also in the *Nativity* on LF 11.

14. The ox and ass in Infancy scenes are discussed by E. Panofsky, *Early Netherlandish Painting*, I, n. 278[1].

15. *Meditations on the Life of Christ*, ed. Ragusa and Green, p. 32f.

16. A radiant Christ in the *Nativity* appears earlier in the triptych of 1367 by

Giusto de Menabuoi in London, National Gallery (S. Bettini, *Giusto de Menabuoi e l'arte del Trecento*, Padua, 1944, fig. 31). The Virgin and midwives on LF 11 also resemble their counterparts in Giusto's *Nativity*.

17. The motif of the Lord holding keys is unusual. He does so in a thirteenth-century fresco of the Majesty of the Apocalypse in the crypt of the Cathedral of Anagni (O. Demus, *Romanesque Mural Painting*, London, 1970, plate opposite p. 32).

18. *Meditations,* ed. Ragusa and Green, pp. 5–9. For a history of the debate, see S. Chew, *The Virtues Reconciled*, Toronto, 1947, pp. 35–68. Professor Chew cites several Books of Hours of the fifteenth and sixteenth centuries in which Virtues in the presence of the Lord accompany or precede the Annunciation. Unlike LF 11v, however, these miniatures include only those Virtues named in the debate (Justice, Truth, Mercy, and Peace). Nor are they associated with representations of the Fall of the Rebel Angels.

The *Fall of the Rebel Angels* precedes the Penitential Psalms on fol. 64v, an inset page in the *Très Riches Heures of Jean, Duke of Berry* (see the publication with commentaries by J. Longnon and R. Cazelles, New York, 1969, no. 65).

19. Bent architectural details like those in the borders of LF 12 do not occur in Giovannino's portion of the Visconti Hours. They are common, however, in the Breviary illuminated by his workshop between 1396 and 1398 (Milan, Biblioteca Trivulziana, lat. 2262).

20. Heads in a Tree of Life occur in an illuminated T (*Te Igitur*) in a Gradual-Sacramentary of the early fourteenth century in Saint Florian, Stiftsbibliothek, ms. III. 205a, fol. 69 (G. Schmidt, *Die Malerschule von St. Florian*, Linz, 1962, pl. 5B).

21. J. Seznec, *The Survival of the Pagan Gods*, New York, 1953, pp. 156–163.

22. Extensive use of silver or silver-like pigments, in addition to gold, characterizes Belbello's part of the Visconti prayer book. For metallic pigments in manuscripts, see S. M. Alexander, "Medieval Recipes Describing the Use of Metals in Manuscripts," *Marsyas*, XII, 1964–1965, pp. 34–51.

23. Although the *Historia* was widely known, Peter Comestor drew on earlier commentators. The motif of the boy directing Lamech's arrow appears in twelfth-century Byzantine Octateuchs, where its textual source must be earlier than the *Historia*. The scene of Lamech killing Cain with an arrow occurs in Italy, as early as Wiligelmo's sculpture on the facade of Modena Cathedral (1099–1106), but here the boy is omitted.

24. The *nodo* and crown with laurel and palm branches occur also in the Duke's Suetonius (Paris, Bibl. nat., ital. 131, fol. 1) and Livy (Paris, Bibl. nat., ital. 118, fol. 1). Both folios are reproduced in Pellegrin, 1969, pls. 110, 111.

25. The sources and history of the motif have been studied by R. Mellinkoff, *The Horned Moses in Medieval Art and Thought*, Berkeley, Los Angeles, London, 1970.

26. The red man or child emerging from the mouth of the Visconti *biscia* is traditionally identified as a Saracen, symbolic of Ottone Visconti's victory in the First Crusade.

27. There is evidence of a Florentine tradition in the fourteenth century for Temperance with a sheathed sword. Temperance binds up her sheathed sword in the Arena Chapel, and she sheathes it in Andrea Pisano's door to the Florentine Baptistery and in the tomb of Francesco Pazzi, in S. Croce.

Bibliography

Giovannino dei Grassi

Arano Cogliati, L., and M. L. Gengaro, *Miniature Lombarde*, Milan (Cassa di Risparmio delle Provincie Lombarde), 1970, pp. 50, 405–409, 421f.

Arslan, E., "Riflessioni sulla pittura gotica 'internazionale' in Lombardia nel tardo Trecento," *Arte Lombarda*, VIII, pt. 2, 1963, pp. 25–66.

Cadei, A., "Giovannino de Grassi nel Taccuino di Bergamo," *Critica d'Arte*, XVII, 109, pp. 17–36.

Meiss, M., *French Painting in the Time of Jean de Berry: The Late Fourteenth Century and the Patronage of the Duke*, London, 1967, pp. 143–146; *The Boucicaut Master*, London, 1968, p. 67f.

Milan, Palazzo Reale, *Arte Lombarda dai Visconti agli Sforza* (exhibition catalogue; entries for manuscripts by R. Cipriani), 1958, pp. 31–35.

Pächt, O., "Early Italian Nature Studies and the Early Calendar Landscape," *Journal of the Warburg and Courtauld Institutes*, XIII, 1950, pp. 13–47.

Taccuino di disegni. Codice della Biblioteca Civica di Bergamo, Bergamo (Banco Piccolo Credito Bergamasco), 1961.

Toesca P., *La pittura e la miniatura nella Lombardia dai più antichi monumenti alla metà del Quattrocento*, Milan, 1912, pp. 294–337 and passim.

White, J., *Art and Architecture in Italy: 1250–1400*, Baltimore, 1966, pp. 383–385, 393f.

Belbello da Pavia

D'Ancona, M. L., *The Wildenstein Collection of Illuminations. The Lombard School*, Florence, 1970, pp. 35–59 (includes an extensive bibliography as well as a list of the manuscripts and numerous single leaves which have been attributed to Belbello).

Milan, Biblioteca Nazionale Braidense, *Mostra di Codici Miniati* (exhibition catalogue), 1970, nos. 31, 32 (catalogued by S. Samek Ludovici).

Milan, Palazzo Reale, *Arte Lombarda dai Visconti agli Sforza* (see bibliography for Giovannino), pp. 75–78.

Pacchioni, G., "Belbello da Pavia e Gerolamo da Cremona miniatori. Un prezioso Messale Gonzaghesco del sec. XV," *L'Arte*, XVIII, 1915, pp. 241–252; 368–372.

Salmi, M., "Contributo a Belbello da Pavia," *Miscellanea Giovanni Galbiati*, Milan, 1951, II, pp. 321–328.

Samek Ludovici S., "Belbello da Pavia," *Bollettino d'arte*, XXXVIII, 1953, pp. 211–224.

Samek Ludovici, S., *Miniature di Belbello da Pavia dalla Bibbia Vaticana e dal Messale Gonzaga di Mantova*, Milan, 1954.

Toesca, P., *La pittura e miniatura nella Lombardia* (see bibliography for Giovannino), 1912, pp. 535–549, 582.

Toesca, P., *L'Uffiziolo Visconteo Landau Finaly donato alla Città di Firenze*, Florence, 1951.

Zeri, F., "Belbello da Pavia: un salterio," *Paragone*, 1950, no. 3, pp. 50–52.